actor. writer. whatever.

All Best,

ako dako press
brooklyn, ny

actor.
writer.
whatever.

(essays on my rise
to the top of the bottom
of the entertainment industry)

mellini kantayya

ISBN-10: 0988466007

ISBN-13: 978-0-9884660-0-5

LCCN: 2012921063

Ako Dako Press
Brooklyn, NY

www.akodakopress.com

For Sean and Teru Lily,

of course

The names of the people in this book have been changed. Or, more accurately, the names of the people on whom these characters are loosely based have been changed. Which brings me to the struggle I had in finding the right genre label for these essays. "Memoir" comes the closest, but it's memoir-*ish*, as some of the essays could also be filed under fiction, creative nonfiction, cultural criticism, or parody. It should be taken in the spirit of listening to an old guy at the end of a smoke-filled bar spinning yarns of his glory days; there's a teensy grain of truth somewhere, but the tales grow taller in the telling. He could care less whether his audience is aware of this. His only goal is to entertain.

My point is: please don't sue me.

Thanks.

contents

introduction:

the plight of the actor, writer, whatever

1

those who can't

8

day jobs and the unutterable

18

i know the secret and it's not worth telling

30

quotable encouragement

45

notes
52

to the author of *the secret*
76

the antisocial network
81

why you frontin'
91

the incredibly sticky, uncomfortable,
complicated, minefield-laden subject of race
99

why my screenplay isn't finished
119

just say no . . . or the curious case
of joan rivers
125

did i peak too soon?
137

what could possibly happen?
154

why do you ask?
170

the memoir rules!
181

about the author
188

acknowledgments
195

actor. writer. whatever.

introduction

the plight
of the actor,
writer, whatever

The Hollywood starlet who was discovered at the mall . . .

The single mother who wrote a Tony Award–winning play while standing in line for food stamps . . .

The indie filmmaker who financed his Sundance hit by selling his blood—one pint at a time . . .

OVERNIGHT SUCCESS STORIES abound, yet at any given time 97 percent of the 120,000 members of the Screen Actors Guild are unemployed. Ninety-five percent of Sundance films don't get distribution. Good

2 | mellini kantayya

novels, poems, and plays sit in dusty desk drawers everywhere. This is the plight of the rank-and-file Actor, Writer, Whatever. These are my people. Fuck those overnight-success freaks.

Worse than tales of the overnight-success freaks are the tales of the "try, try, try again" freaks. These have been taunting Actor, Writer, Whatevers since the dawn of time. The studio executive's report on Fred Astaire's screen test read, "Can't act. Can't sing. Balding. Can dance a little." A newspaper editor fired Walt Disney because "he lacked imagination and had no good ideas." *Gone with the Wind* was rejected thirty-eight times. Blah blah blah blah, blah blah blah. I contend that these stories are lies dreamed up by PR pros who get a perverse thrill from feeding false hope to people who will never "make it," or at least never make it like *that*. It's that same false hope that drove Willy Loman to crash the car.

We're constantly fed a diet of Horatio Alger–esque stories: a little luck, a little pluck, and a dash of talent are all it takes. Take David Sedaris. The program host of Sedaris's 1992 National Public Radio broadcast wrapped up by saying, "David Sedaris worked as an elf at Macy's last year and the year before. He now cleans apartments in New York."

So how did a housecleaner get to read his essay on

NPR's *Morning Edition?* How did that gargantuan leap from point A to point B happen? It's reported he worked a string of odd jobs and was eventually discovered reading his diary in a Chicago club by producer Ira Glass, who then invited him to appear on his weekly radio program. Sedaris later said, "My life just changed completely, like someone waved a magic wand."

I wish someone would wave a magic wand for me and change my life completely. Actually, I would be ecstatic if someone could change my life even a little bit. Maybe they could wave something like a magic toothpick. If I were reading my diary in that club, the most I could hope for would be someone to feel sorry for me and buy me a nice cold Budweiser.

Here's another question: What would have became of David Sedaris if Ira Glass hadn't happened to be in that bar? What would have happened if the magic wand were never waved? Would he have continued bouncing around from odd job to odd job, writing as much as he could while struggling to make rent? Maybe he'd catch a little break here or there. Maybe he'd get published in an obscure literary magazine. Maybe he'd get a steady gig reading his work at one of those out-of-the-way hole-in-the-wall bars with a two-drink minimum. At a party, when a friend was asked, would he or she say, "Oh, that guy? The one slipping hors d'oeuvres into

his public-radio tote bag? That's my friend David . . .
He cleans apartments. He's apparently a writer too."
And would there be the ever-so-slight hint of pity in
their voice when they said it? Would Sedaris's life be a
constant tug of war between making art and making
rent? Would his life be a prolonged, high-effort uphill
climb? Would his life be . . . like *mine*?

"John Henryism" was a term coined by public
health researcher Sherman James to describe the phenomenon of prolonged, high-effort coping with psychological stressors that result in stress-related conditions
such as hypertension. Like the folk hero the syndrome
was named for, the subjects in James's study most likely
to suffer from John Henryism were African American
working-class males who were ambitious and extremely
hard-working.

However, it wasn't the hard work that was deemed
the culprit for the hypertension. It was the subjects'
belief that their hard work would have a positive outcome, that they possessed all the power to achieve their
dreams, and that if they hadn't thus far it was due to
lack of effort. They were resolved to work harder in
the future. The subjects believed they were in total control of their destiny, without acknowledging the role of
luck, time, money, or the challenges of the social and
economic class into which they were born. It wasn't the

hard work that made them sick. It was the dream that it would all pay off one day.

The day I read about this study, I could not stop turning over the similarities between the John Henrys and my own life as an Actor, Writer, Whatever. Though mine was a self-made purgatory, the study resonated so deeply with me that I started to cry as I explained it to my husband while we were walking to Trader Joe's. I had been at this for ten years. No screenplays had been produced. Writing contests and grant applications had never resulted in more than "finalist" or "second place." My credits at the time included low-budget indie films and a small role on a soap opera.

If I divorced myself from hope, if I divorced myself from emotion, if I looked at my dreams in terms of logic and statistics and probabilities, I was most likely not to make it. And my idea of making it was seemingly obtainable: to be able to support myself without having a day job, earning as much as my husband, the public-school teacher.

I didn't want to be a John Henry or a Don Quixote or a character in any tragic tale, but at that moment I felt I was one. I cried. I'm crying as I write this even now. I apologized to my husband because even in knowing success might never happen, in fully accepting my life and career would probably always be a struggle, I wasn't going to quit. My employment ambitions would remain day jobs that would accommodate writing time and auditions. I apologized for the income I was not going to earn and for just how much harder our lives would be because, despite this revelation, nothing was going to change. Heroin addicts can get clean. I never would.

I kept crying and apologizing, and my darling mensch of a husband turned to me, looked into my eyes, and said, "Are you getting your period or something?"

"No! I am not getting my period!" (Though maybe I was.) "Have you heard a word I've said?"

"Yeah, but . . . does it really matter? I mean, it's just what you do."

And he was right. It is just what I do. Just what I am. Like my being short, there is nothing I can do about it. It doesn't matter if I am good or bad at it, successful or unsuccessful, rich, poor, or destined to die facedown in a gutter. No matter how miserable the circumstance, *it's just what I do.*

I wish I could say it was this lightbulb moment that changed my life, that I found peace and went on *The Oprah Show* to talk about it or even didn't go on *The Oprah Show* but *still* felt all peaceful and shit (not being on *The Oprah Show* and *still* finding inner peace is pretty fucking peaceful—it's what the ancient

Hindus called the *Vedanta Avayunā*, literally "reaching a higher ground of peace and understanding without being on *The Oprah Show*"), but, alas, I wasn't any more or less peaceful. I felt pretty much the same. Like John Henry or Don Quixote, I tell a story. *I tell stories* and I would wake up the next morning and not do anything differently . . . except write this book.

| those who can't

EVERY NOW AND THEN, when I feel hopelessly stalled, I Google myself to make sure I still exist. No matter how often I do this, I'm still surprised to find myself alive and well on the Internet. A lapse in forward progress has not erased me from the world completely. I watch a video of my acting clips. I read my IMDb (Internet Movie Database) page and a mention of me on a soap opera blog. Somewhere in the thirteenth search page, I find some old articles on the film festival I founded. This practice is a nice reminder that even when my career is moving at a glacial pace, it is still moving. It is not sad and pathetic.

What is sad and pathetic, however, is when I start

Googling other people: an ex-boyfriend (a successful theater actor, but not one IMDb credit—ha ha), someone from an old acting class (wow, she's doing quite well—moving on). I Google Jack Oyster, an acting teacher from college. According to the theater department staff bios, in the years since I graduated, he moved all the way up from assistant professor to associate professor. I take a moment to imagine him miserable. *Who's Afraid of Virginia Woolf?* miserable.

My first encounter with Professor Jack Oyster, or "Pro Jack," as his students affectionately nicknamed him, happened when I was coming off the high of being a minor campus celebrity. I played "The Stud" in Eric Bogosian's *Sex, Drugs, and Rock and Roll.* Another professor directed it. I had enjoyed working with him so much I declared theater as my minor. I felt like I was on a roll and couldn't wait to audition for Pro Jack's production of *Tartuffe*, by Molière (one of my favorites, especially the Richard Wilbur translations). All the theater department darlings adored Pro Jack. They wrapped themselves around him like kudzu. I showed up at the audition prepped and ready to land the role of Dorine.

His audition questionnaire was more extensive than the other professor's. Along with contact information and class schedule, the form included questions like "Can you cry on cue?" "Are you willing to do a homosexual love scene?" and "Will you do partial or full nudity?" I'm pretty sure nudity was not allowed in university productions and there's no homosexuality in *Tartuffe*. I guessed Pro Jack wanted to ascertain whether we were fully committed to our craft—willing to take our art to the limits. I checked "yes" to all (though I cannot cry on cue).

I gave what I think was a solid audition. He and the student stage manager laughed in all the right places. They seemed engaged throughout. Afterward, Pro Jack smiled and thanked me for auditioning and seemed sincere. All positive signs, so I have no idea why I then asked, "Will this be colorblind cast?"

He hesitated slightly before answering, "I don't believe in colorblind casting."

Except for confirming that I had very good intuition, I had wasted my time. He had basically just told me point-blank that I would be denied participation in a school-sponsored activity due to race. Instead of complaining to the administration or contacting the ACLU, I signed up for Pro Jack's class the next semester. I don't know whether it was masochistic leanings or youthful idealism or both, but I honestly believed I could turn him around, thus breaking down the door for actors of color everywhere. Maybe they'll put me on a t-shirt like Che Guevara or César Chávez. Besides, the theater

department was small. I could not complete the require-
ments of my minor without taking one of his classes.

The first day of class he handed out the syllabus
and gave a brief lecture about ACT-ING (I use the caps
and the hyphen in an attempt to portray a Boston Brah-
min accent, à la John Houseman in *The Paper Chase.*
"Act," and its derivatives, were the only words he said
this way). He said the role of the ACT-OR was akin to
that of the shaman in ancient cultures. The ACT-OR
is also a mystic, transporting the audience into another
world and ultimately on to enlightenment. The chal-
lenge of the class would be to push our bodies and souls
to explore the outer edges of our psyches, even parts
we did not want anyone, including ourselves, to see. I
started to question my future ambitions. I wanted to tell
stories and play make-believe, not get into therapy or be
salacious for its own sake.

But ACT-ING 101 began innocently enough. The
first unit was improvisation. Pro Jack would throw out a
situation and we'd have to improv, not with another student, but with him. "Fun!" the kudzu clamored. I am
not a "Fun!" person (yep, not even in college), so I tried
extra, extra hard. Which, of course, is the antithesis of
fun. Still, I did manage to be wry, witty, quick, but Pro
Jack didn't seem appreciative of wry, witty, quick. I'd
flow with whatever scenario he'd throw out. When the

six-minute timer went off, I sat down, and . . . he'd have no comment until after the next student had performed. He then would gush over that student, especially if he or she had done something provocative, perhaps the mentioning of abortion or a scatological issue. I was relieved when we moved on to the next unit: theater games.

I remember one game in particular. We'd all stand in a circle. Pro Jack would call out a single word, and we had to "act out" that word. "Rage," he called out, and we'd all stomp around with clenched fists. "Joke," he called out. I held my gut and keeled over with forced laughter while others pretended to fall on a banana peel or tell a joke. "Sex," he called out. I froze. What the hell was I supposed to do here?!? I was a college student and, so far, only had experience with college boys. So I did what I knew. I lay down, politely smiled, and waited patiently for the awkwardness to end.

I didn't have the nerve to check out what the guys in the class were doing, but most of the girls were doing pretty much the same thing—except Krissie. Krissie had already set herself apart from the rest of the students. Not only did Pro Jack rave about everything she did (it was Krissie who brought up abortion in her improv), but unlike most of us who showed up to class in sweats and a ponytail, she'd be dressed in the latest trend and full makeup, as if central casting had sent over a middle-aged man's fantasy of a coed.

Krissie was taking the game very seriously. With "sex," she arched her back, closed her eyes, and undulated softly and rhythmically without the slightest self-consciousness. I'd heard she had just broken up with her boyfriend, and I briefly wondered if he was still available—then I noticed Pro Jack. Watching her. With *that* look—a look that should not be employed by a professor observing a student. The exercise continued until Pro Jack realized I was watching him. He quickly averted his eyes and called out a new word: "Shame."

Freud wasn't full of shit after all.

The culmination of the class, and one-third of our final grade, was a scene we would prepare with an assigned partner. As Pro Jack passed out the scenes, I wondered what I would wind up with, given his stated opposition to colorblind casting. Being the only Indian American in class, would I be acting out all the parts of the *Ramayana* myself? No. Pro Jack took the word "colorblind" quite literally. To him it meant *color*, not heritage (no one cast in *Tartuffe* was 100 percent French—I checked). I was partnered with the only African American in class, and we would be performing a scene from August Wilson's *Fences*.

My scene partner was a nice enough guy. Bryan was a chemistry major, who, like me, was working his way through college. Unlike me, he never intended to pursue acting and was taking the class as an easy elective. However, memorizing his lines or meeting me for rehearsals proved not so easy when the weight of his full course load and job responsibilities pressed against him. He blew me off half a dozen times, and though he was always apologetic, I got increasingly frustrated.

Doing well was important to me—not only for my GPA and future ambitions, but because I wanted to prove something to Professor Jack Oyster. The more it seemed he didn't like me, the more I wanted his approval. Instead of embodying the shaman, I embodied the other actor archetype: the one wrought with insecurities who overcompensates by putting herself in the spotlight, demanding attention, appreciation, and applause—all while wearing a disguise.

Finally, when Bryan started hinting at dropping the class, I brought my troubles to Pro Jack, hoping that for once he would embody the super-cool professor persona all the other students saw. I hoped he would empathize and reassign a monologue for the final. He refused, saying, "In the theater you have to deal with the circumstances which you are given."

I thought maybe he didn't fully understand my plight. "But—"

"I'm sorry. You'll have to manage. My office hours are over, so if you'll excuse me."

I called Bryan in a panic, begging him not to drop the class. He eventually relented, but could rehearse for only half an hour before the final. We were going to have to wing it.

And wing it we did. Throughout, Bryan laughed nervously with every line he dropped, snuck a peek at the photocopied script in his back pocket, and then laughed even more uncomfortably as he continued. I struggled to soldier on. I strained against Bryan's schoolgirl giggling to bring the appropriate downtrodden world-weariness to my character's lines. It took every ounce of resolve not to sit on the floor, bury my face in my hands, and cry a big ugly cry. My final grade for the semester was a C–. Bryan's was a B. I changed my minor from theater to dance the next day.

I still have no idea why Jack had it in for me. Maybe it was because I forced him to confess his politically incorrect colorblind policy. Maybe it was because I caught him ogling Krissie. Maybe it was for reasons unknown even to him. But he did enough damage to swear me off acting. If it was all a big mind fuck, I wanted no part of it.

I cannot say why I returned to acting after college. Before I moved to New York I found myself auditioning at a major regional theater in front of a celebrated director, for a Pulitzer Prize–winning playwright's world premiere. All the roles were cast out of New York, except for two chorus roles open to locals. I landed one. I played an Eastern European Jew. It was colorblind cast.

Remembering all this, my baser, more *schäden-freude*-tinged self clicks around the search engine to be sure that Jack Oyster has not escaped the ivory tower. Don't get me wrong; I deeply believe that teaching is the noblest of professions. I got a very good education. Being at a state college, most of my professors were focused on teaching rather than on getting published. Many were adjuncts, out in the world writing novels and poems while sharing their knowledge with us. A great sense of camaraderie existed there. I even played in the English majors versus English professors softball league. Jack Oyster was the exception, not the rule. So why is he the first thing I think of when I think of my college days?

I'm perversely satisfied when I can't find one acting or directing credit to his name outside of university productions. I do find out that his mother gave a huge financial gift to his own alma mater, an Ivy League school. She's quoted in the university's newsletter: "In his senior year, Jack wrote an original play based on his student experiences. It captured the prestigious University Student Playwright's Award. I remember Jack calling to tell us, 'Can you believe it? I'm starting out on top.'"

For some in academia teaching is, in and of itself, a rewarding pursuit. I suspect this was not the case for Professor Oyster, that as a senior in college, at a time when we all feel we have the future figured out and are certain our lives will be charmed, magical, and just oh so lovely, Jack fancied himself the next Sam Shepard. He thought he'd be a lauded playwright and a fine actor, more likely to be interviewed by *Theater Week* than by *Entertainment Tonight*, admired by an educated class of people who were the arbiters of good taste, culture, and intellectual discourse. I'll never know what circumstances led Jack Oyster to teach at my decidedly not-prestigious school after his early successes.

I emerge from my Internet wanderings disappointed in myself, more for the wasted time than for anything else. The common wisdom is that no one can make you feel bad about yourself without your permission, but screw that. When you encounter someone who has been disappointed in life, has not processed that disappointment and gone through the painstaking labor of changing it into growth . . . *someone* has to pay, and it might as well be you.

day jobs and
the unutterable

THE ISAMU NOGUCHI coffee table. It's the Mona Lisa of coffee tables, the most well-designed and easily recognizable coffee table in the world. It's also expensive: about fifteen hundred dollars. My friend Chuck has one. It sits (under an inch of dust, empty takeout containers, and an ashtray overflowing with cigarette butts and a few nail clippings) in his co-op apartment, which he owns in a lovely doorman building in the West Village; where a price tag of three-quarters of a million dollars for an apartment the same size as my college dorm room is the deal of the century.

Chuck is under thirty. Six days out of three hundred and sixty-five he works as an actor. The rest of the time he works part-time as a waiter. When I was a bartender, I barely scraped together my half of the rent for a three-hundred-square-foot rent-controlled apartment. My bedroom was so small I slept in a makeshift loft on a sliver of a futon, my face six inches from the ceiling—like those little cubbyholes Tokyo businessmen sleep in. Or a coffin.

I lived in Manhattan when I first moved to the city. I spent time with Kelly, someone I had casually known back home, despite not liking her. Well, I sort of liked her. She had something I was attracted to. It was an attraction based on opposites. I was dark and wry and dry. She was shiny and bright and blonde. I was a thinker, an *overthinker.* She was a doer. She did dinner out. She did men. She did whatever she damn well pleased the instant it occurred to her without the slightest concern for consequences. We both had the same job . . . sort of. She was a hostess at a restaurant and I was a bartender. I would have assumed bartenders earned more than hostesses, but she was living so much larger than I was. She was enrolled at a highly reputed acting studio, one that you had to get a recommendation to even audition for (she knew someone who pulled a few strings). She could afford the exorbitant tuition. She could afford an apartment on Prince Street. She could afford the constant influx of clothes, cosmetics, and accoutrements in rope-handle bags from SoHo boutiques that made their way onto every square inch of her hand-woven rugs and retro modern furniture. She dined at the latest hot spots and afterward, the velvet ropes always parted for her when she arrived at the clubs. She made me feel like a tremendous loser.

Others besides Kelly made me feel as if I either was not working hard enough or was unlucky in a city whose air is thick with the desire and will to get lucky. Another friend, Beth-Ann, had a spacious studio on the Upper West Side. Now, the apartment thing can be tricky because it's not always an indicator of wealth. Sometimes a person lucks into a rent-controlled situation like I first did. Beth-Ann came to New York to act, supporting herself by working as a makeup artist a few times a month. I wasn't sure how much part-time makeup artists made. She lived beyond my means while never giving a passing thought to money, yet she'd landed in New York at the same time as I did. One day, Beth-Ann inadvertently illuminated the landscape for me. She was talking about a friend of hers whose parents had cut her off after she had graduated from Bennington. "I have a real problem with that. I mean, who does that? My daddy is real good to me. There's no way I could make it in the city without his help."

I didn't take her comment as arrogant or clueless. I was grateful for being released from my feelings of inadequacy (at least in this regard). I was the exception, it seemed, surviving in this city without any help, and that was something to be proud of. Now I finally saw how other dues-paying Actor, Writer, Whatevers were affording lifestyles befitting associates at corporate law firms. If I had first moved to Brooklyn, where all the other Actor, Writer, Whatevers were migrating at the time, instead of Manhattan, I would have been spared this skewed version of reality. If I had been the seasoned New Yorker I am now, it would have been clear (though a telltale sign should have been the dusty disheveled apartments with high-end furniture: up-by-your-bootstraps people bled for what they have and keep that shit clean). Chuck, Kelly, and Beth-Ann had *Gelt HaMeforash.*

The Hebrew phrase *Shem HaMeforash* translates to "The Unspeakable Name of God," meaning God's name is so sacred it's unutterable. In New York, money, or *gelt*, goes the same way as God, thus *Gelt HaMeforash.* Those with *Gelt HaMeforash* maim, crush, and castrate the egos of those of us without it. We wonder if we're lacking their talent or gumption, when all we're really lacking is their money.

New York is teeming with *Gelt HaMeforash*; a parent-purchased apartment, a trust fund, or a monthly lifestyle subsidy check. I don't respect anyone less for

having it. Honest, I don't. (No, really.) Faulting someone for having and using unspoken money is like faulting a pro basketball player for being tall. *Ac-cent-tchu-
ate the positive*, as Ella Fitzgerald sang. We all have to
use what we've got. And what I wound up getting was
my big daddy, Goldie.

My big daddy Goldie was Goldman Sachs along
with various other investment banks. Bartending had
gotten too rough. I was sick of the smoke (you could
smoke in bars in New York then). I was sick of getting
hit on by the ugly, drunk guys (and not getting hit on
by the cute, sober ones). I was sick of hauling trash to
the curb at four in the morning, getting home by four-
thirty, and not being able to fall asleep until seven, with
an audition inevitably scheduled for ten a.m. I slept
all day and couldn't get into the groove of writing. I
needed a day job that wasn't a *commitment* commitment. I needed flexibility. I needed to make the rent. I
needed to temp.

This was during a lush economic time. I could
type (sort of). I had half a brain (sort of). This and a
pulse, even a weak one, were all the agency required.
They could barely keep up with the rising demand
for temporary administrative help. Temps became a
Manhattan accessory, like a Prada bag or Jimmy Choo
shoes. Credit default swaps schmaps . . . I'm certain the

overuse of temps is what caused the financial crash.

No matter what company they sent me to, the days were all the same. I would arrive in reception and wait seven to fourteen minutes until someone would arrive and show me through the maze of cubicles to my seat. She would give a brief explanation of how the phones worked, whom I would be working for, and directions to the ladies' room, which were useless because I would always get lost. And then the "job" began. I would sit there. And sit there. And sit there. They didn't need me. It was all about image. I was window dressing. A trophy temp. The investment banker, or whomever I was temping under, needed to seem so important that he could not go one minute without an assistant. The other administrative assistants needed to seem so busy that they couldn't possibly handle taking over for someone else for a whole day.

This gave me time to write, memorize scenes for acting class, balance my checkbook, read. If I had an audition I considered it my lunch break, even if it was at nine-thirty a.m. An additional benefit was that working at a different location every day allowed me to wear the same outfit on consecutive days, thus keeping my professional wardrobe expenditures to a minimum and preserving my meager budget for going-out-at-night wear. My friend Vikas worked in finance and pointed out another benefit. "Kantayya, you should be checking out these corporate cafeterias. Some of the best cuisine in the city." He was practically giddy.

"Really?"

"Yeah, and the real test of the quality of a corporate cafeteria is the lemon meringue pie."

In case you're wondering, Goldman Sachs did not have the best lemon meringue pie. That honor went to the Midtown Citicorp building.

After I took my seat the nine hours would stretch out before me. The phone would ring five to seven times. I would type one letter. File four folders. The rest of the time I would work on my own stuff. At three o'clock I would be interrupted by the temp in the adjacent cubicle, who would seize an opportunity usually limited to being seated next to a stranger on a plane. I became a pro bono therapist, an open ear to vent to about her boyfriend, opera career, or children. The latter was rare. Usually the temps were about my age and involved in the arts: writers, actors, dancers, opera singers. Lots of opera singers. The typing pool at Lehman Brothers could have put on a decent production of *The Pirates of Penzance*. (Frankly, I can't remember if it was Lehman Brothers or J.P. Morgan, but there's no more Lehman Brothers, so who's gonna call me on it?)

My office temp days are long behind me, but I still get soul-crushing reminders of the people I've worked with. They're all around me, whether at the theater, in the banner ad on the website I just clicked to, or in the movie or TV show I'm watching. Several times a week, usually when I am suffering through a painfully long period of rejection and unemployment, there they are, mocking me—pleasant little reminders that others have risen in the ranks and I've been left behind. Most of them likely still need to work day jobs, but this fact never enters my ruminations. One fellow temp, someone about whom I distinctly remember thinking, *this guy will never make it*, has done a series of pharmaceutical ads. I picture the lovely co-op he's purchased for himself on Central Park West. I force myself to reread my résumé to remind myself that I am not a complete loser. I am not a complete failure. I'm not I'm not I'm not.

Eventually, after bouncing for a while from company to company, I wound up with a perma-temp gig. Perma-temps are temporary workers with no end date of engagement. I landed at Goldman Sachs, working for a senior vice president. He was nuts—a good nuts—and an anomaly in the investment banking world. He was gruff, swore like a sailor, and didn't talk as much as bark. And he was smart. Real smart. Not the

I-grew-up-going-to-fancy-private-schools-Ivy-League-all-the-way-to-MBA smart. He was *born-in-a-resettle-ment-camp-parents-immigrated-to-Brooklyn-after-World-War-II-up-by-my-bootstraps-well-educated-and-have-savvy-you-can't-buy* smart. He was the first person I temped for whom I genuinely liked and respected.

He came in very early every morning, before everyone else, worked steadily, efficiently, and productively as long as he needed to, and then went home. This was a rare thing at investment banks and rarer among the young associates. They *lived* at work. It was more part of the corporate culture than a necessity of the job. The associates would roll in around ten, deal with whatever their vice president handed them, eat lunch at their desks, work until three . . . and then who knows what the hell they did until the evening, besides come by my desk to shoot the shit.

I hated this. It was a far worse fate than having your ear bent by an administrative assistant or a fellow temp. My VP kept me busy, but only in spurts. I wanted to use my downtime to write, not chat with twenty-four-year-olds with expense accounts. In spite of these intrusions I wrote an entire play while at Goldman Sachs. It was produced Way-Off-Broadway and enjoyed a sold-out run.

Certainly some of the associates were interesting people. Those people did not come by my desk to shoot the shit. It was the other breed: take a birth into social advantage, isolate that person in an upper-class suburb, send them to an elite university followed by an even more elite MBA program, and voilà! You have a torturously boring person. Especially at three p.m., when you're plugging through the second act of the play you're surreptitiously writing at work.

Thankfully, the stream of chatty associates usually stopped around five. A few would head over to the gym—but just women. The men knew that as investment bankers, they were destined to be rich, which meant they could get as fat as they wanted and still get a hot wife.

I did the evening shift a couple of times a week. Time and a half plus free dinner, to sit there in the event that someone might need administrative help between the hours of five and nine. Multiply me by the twenty temps on the floor, multiply that by forty floors, multiply that by three buildings, then multiply that by twenty countries. That's how much money just one investment bank was spending on evening temporary workers on the off chance something needed to be faxed. The modern banking version of the Roman orgy before the fall of the empire.

I milked it for all I could, but eventually I quit. The atmosphere became, well, sad: night after night watching associates eating dinner together in the conference room, and then going out for drinks with those same coworkers, living the high life with the same type of people they had lived the high life with in kindergarten, taking sixteen hours to do a job that could have been done in nine. The bonds among them were interchangeable, built on proximity not affection. If they moved on to another department or company, they would seamlessly swap the old friends for the new ones.

Even sadder were the thirty- or forty-year-old VPs passing the time in their offices or by making small talk with the associates and temps, all to avoid going home and interacting with their wives and children. They left at nine p.m. to commute an hour and a half to Westchester or Connecticut, which left them just about eight hours of sleep before the next hour-and-a-half commute. I guess for some people it's worth it. Being rich. I think I'd rather have time than money. A life is just units of time.

I quit and became a freelance bookkeeper. Less time more money, but I'll skip that part. No anecdotes there. Nobody loves the bookkeeper. When I quit for day job number four, no one cared. The coworkers at an architectural firm barely looked up from their desks to wave goodbye. The high school intern was there three months and got a cake. I was there for five *years*. Nobody loves the bookkeeper.

Now I'm a certified fitness instructor and personal trainer. I aced the six-hour test. I intuitively know how the body works and how to make it perform efficiently. I've been working out and dancing my whole life. It's my most logical day job to date, and I should have been doing this all along. It comes naturally to me.

I am certain that, eventually, I will quit.

Sometimes while teaching, I look out and think, *Why can't this be enough? I'm confident here. I'm good at it. I enjoy it. Why can't this be enough? Why can't I just be a personal trainer? Why can't this plus my family, friends, and hobbies be enough?* It's a great job. I would have a full life and never again feel audition anxiety. I wouldn't feel unbearably restless when not involved in a project. I could stop obsessively reading scripts. I wouldn't lose time rehearsing for auditions for roles I will never be cast in. I would be free of my secret wish for *Gelt HaMeforash* to release me from day jobs forever.

My class is on its fourth set of crunches when I realize I may not be all that different from that investment banker on his long commute back to the office, back to the gilded cage, too blinded by the glittering bars to see the world beyond.

i know the secret and it's not worth telling

I HAVE A RECURRING supporting role on a soap opera. It is thoroughly enjoyable work and I love it. Do not mock soap operas. Just don't. The narrative is stunningly complex, thus demanding the oft-mocked style of performance that broadly indicates, rather than providing emotionally nuanced characterizations. The genre was born in the early days of American radio and has made its way onto television sets all over the world. In Latin America, soaps tend to be closed, meaning there is a primary conflict (usually involving a musta-chioed villain), which is eventually resolved. In Amer-ica, soaps are open-ended. The writers must have the skill to have one tidal wave swell as another reaches the shore of denouement, while yet another is swept out to return at an unanticipated time (all without stooping to the device of mustachio-ing the villain). The popularity of soap operas in Latin America and the Middle East is waxing while viewership in the United States is waning, but I will always maintain that this is one area where American craftsmanship is still superior. Do not mock soap operas. It's un-American.

Whether a background player (euphemism for "extra"), a bit part like mine, or a superstar with a front-burner storyline, all soap roles require a great deal of focus and stamina. For all the hand-to-forehead melodrama in front of the camera, there's no room for it behind the camera. It's a highly professional work environment, a well-oiled machine where everyone, cast and crew alike, must have their roles down pat. The pace is exhilarating. In one day they shoot as many pages of dialogue as an indie film shoots in twenty-one days, or a studio feature shoots in months or even years. No small feat.

My day starts with a brief rehearsal, then I hustle off to hair and makeup, a quick stop at the wardrobe department, and then . . . I wait. There's usually downtime—a slow mile between sprints. The day players and under-fives (people with under five lines) wait in a shared dressing room, passing time before springing to action. Sometimes this can be a lot of fun: sharing stories with interesting compatriots. Sometimes I'm stuck in the room with a weirdo.

One such day, there were three of us in the dressing room. I was playing a nurse. Another actress was playing a cop. The third actress was playing a body double for a character in a coma. The character had become comatose after the regular actress playing her did not renew her contract. The coma was the perfect plot device to employ while deciding whether to recast the character, kill her off, or keep her in the coma indefinitely, leaving open the option of waking her in the future . . . perhaps after her soul mate had finally moved on and was a nanosecond from getting remarried (I empathize with the imaginary caterer, being left with one hundred beautifully arranged smoked salmon canapés that will spoil within the hour).

We had made our introductions in the rehearsal hall and retired to our communal dressing room. The cop promptly commandeered the couch, laid her iPod on her stomach, inserted earphones, and closed her eyes. The body double took out a book. I unpacked my yarn and crochet hook. We had at least an hour to wait. At any moment, small talk would commence, and within six seconds I would be able to determine if there would be the chemistry for a grand ol' summer camp time (and, later, the traditional unfulfilled promise to stay in touch), or if I would be counting down scenes in the can until I was mercifully called on set.

"What are you making?" the body double asked me.

"Oh, this? Arm warmers."

She touched my yarn. "Soft. I love the color."

"Thanks . . . so what are you reading?"

"*The Power.* By the woman who wrote *The Secret. The Secret* was amazing, but this is the book you want. It's my third time reading it. Totally changed my life."

"Yeah?"

"Oh, yeah! I wouldn't be working like I am, or even have my agent without it. I just quit my day job!"

I followed the rules of small talk and matched her enthusiasm. "Wow! You quit your day job? Congratulations! How'd you do it? Did you get a commercial?"

"No."

"Are you a series regular somewhere?"

"No."

"A Lort Theatre gig?"

"No. Just Off-Off-Broadway stuff."

"So, how'd you do it?"

"I just quit. I needed that day job money to dry up. That money was the money of small thinking. Having bigger thoughts for myself opened up the universe's will for me to earn a living just through acting."

An ethereal glow lit her face. "I took the leap and the net appeared."

Now the pseudo-napping earphone cop girl perked up. She apparently wasn't asleep and had been listening the whole time. I made a mental note to remember the trick. (Forget the magic cloak: someone should tell Harry Potter that all it takes to become invisible is earphones.) But now she couldn't contain herself and gave up the ruse. "But how?!?"

"I just did."

"But how?" we chimed.

"I just did."

We went a couple more rounds of "But how?" "I just did," until finally the cop and I exchanged a covert look, rolled our eyes, and let it go. It was clear we weren't going to get the step-by-step process explained to us in any detail whatsoever.

This wasn't the first conversation I'd had like this, and sadly it won't be the last. *The Secret* and the like have replaced Scientology as the "it" religion for the entertainment industry. Successful Actor, Writer, Whatevers and hacks alike can talk about this power-of-attraction stuff as if it's science. As certain as gravity and hot air rising.

I stumble upon this thinking at the most unexpected times . . . for example, at a marketing and branding seminar. The program was "Actors: Light Your Way!" I didn't take the cheesy title as a sign of things to come. Seminar titles are cheesy by nature, regardless of the content's value. This seminar came highly recommended by several people I respected, and thus far my career focus had been on art and not commerce. I wanted to be enlightened as to why I wasn't making a livable wage as an Actor, Writer, Whatever and get myself "out there." *This will be my magic wand. Everything will be different after today.*

The beginning of the seminar was indeed promising. The presentation room looked professional and marketing-y. The speaker—we'll call him Rick—was confident, charismatic, and well-coiffed: exactly the way I'd want a marketing seminar presenter to look. Rick's initial premise grabbed me from the jump: actors are basically rudderless when it comes to branding themselves and need to "light the way" of their career paths. *Right on, Rick*, I thought. Actors need a laser beam focus on the roles they play well rather than spinning their wheels to get any and every job that comes down the pike. *Right on, Rick.* We start out in the world as babies who see the world as perfect, then we have a ground zero moment that shatters that illusion, then we have a compensation fantasy that drives our behavior in an attempt to return the world back to that perfect place, and that compensation fantasy defines the character type we should be pursuing. *Right on—What? That doesn't make any sense.*

At first Rick was killing me softly with his song. Then he was just killing me. I started to wiggle uncomfortably in my chair and couldn't continue to follow. What I thought was going to be a marketing and branding seminar, rooted in the tangible material world of the flesh, turned out to be a bend-the-universe-to-your-will seminar with a few marketing tips thrown in.

Apparently, I was the only disappointed person in the room. Everyone else seemed wide-eyed, riveted, even grateful. I was the only person in the room who did not sign up for the three-hundred-and-twenty-five-dollar private session to unearth my ground zero moment and discover my true character type.

Do I sound self-righteous? Doth I protest too much? Doth I really?

Okay. Fine. I admit it: I've done it. Not fork over three hundred and twenty-five dollars to find my ground zero moment. (I, very often, am a moron. But I, more often, am cheap. Three hundred and twenty-five dollars to relive a childhood trauma? Thanks, but no.) But I'll cop to the fact that I was, shall we say, a New Age dabbler before *The Secret* came into entertainment industry vogue. *What you visualize will manifest. Create your own reality.* The problem with creating your own reality is that the only person living in it is you.

It's all so understandably seductive, and I was slowly and systematically seduced. After all, the theory stems from solid science. *Nature abhors a vacuum—create a space and nature will rush to fill it. Everything is made of magnetically charged atoms that are always in a state of attraction. Matter is influenced by its environment.* These principles have been proven true but were formed to explain much larger phenomena than paying off credit cards, meeting a new boy, or landing an audition. But after reading a book or two that laid out the most logical of arguments, I couldn't help but ignore the original context and intent.

I started with creative visualizations, which aren't so hocus pocus when taken with the appropriate grain of salt. Cancer patients do it to battle the disease, visualizing the chemotherapy incinerating unwanted invaders. Dancers do it, visualizing every nuance of the choreography in the wings before placing a foot onstage. Professional athletes do it, visualizing the ball's perfect landing in the glove. At best (when within the realm of possibility) visualizations are highly effective; at worst, they're a gateway drug to New Age addiction.

I began imagining my writing projects come to fruition. I began imagining myself relaxed and fully enjoying the audition experience. And all would have been fine and lovely if I'd stopped there. But I didn't. I forgot the old adage about too much of a good thing. An apple a day will keep the doctor away, but nothing but apples all day every day will give you diarrhea.

I moved on to affirmations.

The philosophy behind daily affirmations is that we already run a continuous inner monologue that determines our outlook and, thus, our behavior. The monologue can be positive (an affirmation) or negative (negation? deflation? defamation?). Affirmations are simply a way of actively choosing a positive monologue. When they are repeated daily, the subconscious picks up on the new attitude and, although it may initially rebel, eventually believes the affirmations as truths. Behavioral changes in line with the new beliefs happen effortlessly, and society at large (or the universe, if you will) also senses the change. In turn, one's life is transformed.

I composed a series of affirmations for myself: *I now earn six figures solely through my creative endeavors* (I should have said six figures *without* a decimal point); *I am a confident person, full of grace and style and wit* (I am not); *I now have a pied-à-terre in Paris* (hey, if I'm doing this, why not?). I also threw in affirmations for specific acting gigs I wanted, a laptop with more memory, and a few others far too embarrassing to mention.

Strictly adhering to the rules, I composed each affirmation in the present tense, using only positive language. Negative language evokes negative feelings and therefore negative outcomes. The present tense creates the belief that the affirmation is an established fact and not a longing for the future, in which case it would be the longing that would be affirmed and achieved instead of the goal itself. Simple and logical, right?

I started slow. I made each declaration once or twice a day. Occasionally, I'd write each down five times. This took up no more than ten minutes at a time. But as nothing seemed to be changing, I got it in my head that I was just not doing my affirmations often enough and with the zeal required to make real changes. I dedicated more and more time to performing the incantations. I'd repeat them on the treadmill and walking to the subway. Once on the subway, I'd write down the affirmations over and over until I eventually had notebooks upon notebooks full of *I now earn six figures solely through my creative endeavors. I am a confident person, full of grace and style and wit.*

This creative-visualization, positive-thinking, affirmation stuff became all I thought about. It's a logical marriage for an Actor, Writer, Whatever since our gains and successes are more out of our control than we'd like to admit. It's a field where talent and hard work don't necessarily cut it. Who wouldn't refuse to believe that the statistics apply to them? Who doesn't want to believe that they're special? (My hand waves in the air—*I do! I do!*) It is just a matter of time before the universe discovers and rewards our specialness, and believing in that "fact" wholeheartedly will console us and save us time.

But the strangest thing happened: I didn't feel consoled. Instead of the delicious thrill of being on the brink of realizing all my dreams, I felt generally ill at ease and increasingly irritable. For one thing, I was spending more time on affirmations than on my creative work—the very work that wholly engaged my mind and spirit and gave me a sense of contentment.

Another reason for my ever-present agita was that affirmations share the same flaws as the self-esteem movement: contrary to popular belief, thousands of studies have shown that there is absolutely no causal relationship between high self-esteem and success in school, work, or relationships. In fact, people with high self-esteem are *more* likely to become alcoholics, not less. After a while, children of over-praising parents get the subtler message that they're deficient and *need* to be built up. Or the praise is so frequent and over-the-top that they doubt its sincerity and grow to distrust the praiser—which, in the case of affirmations, is yourself.

After all, if all these statements (in the positive, present tense) were true, wouldn't you be out living a fabulous life instead of gassing yourself up all the time?

This is why the Stuart Smalley skits on *Saturday Night Live* were so funny. When Stuart tells his reflection in the mirror, "I'm good enough, I'm smart enough, and doggone it, people like me," the audience immediately intuits, *he's not good enough, he's not smart enough, nobody likes him.*

This all dawned on me one beautiful summer day when my then fiancé and I were hiking outside the city. We were excited about getting married. As we walked along the trail, we chatted about some of the practicalities of blending our lives. He started mentally calculating the cost of our new apartment and our monthly expenses: "So how much exactly does your bookkeeping take in a month?" These conversations between newlyweds-to-be are often a bit sticky, but they're especially sticky when half of the couple has brainwashed herself and can't bear to state reality as it is, only as she wants it to be.

I knew we needed to have the finances conversation, but I didn't want to undo all my creative visualizations and affirmations. I had "worked" so hard and didn't want to jinx myself. I *couldn't* jinx myself. Until then I had kept my rituals to myself. Some part of me

knew I was actin' all crazy, but I feared that if I admit-
ted to the possibility I might still need a day job by the
time we were married, I would die a bookkeeper.

"I'm not going to work as a bookkeeper." My voice
sounded strange to me, as if someone else was speaking.

"What? What are you going to do?"

"I'm going to earn a living as an actor and writer."

"Yeah, but that isn't enough to live on right now,
is it?"

"No, but it will be then."

He knit his brow. We had just signed a lease on a
new apartment. He was starting grad school and made
a humble public-school teacher's salary. We would
never meet our expenses on the one to three grand a
year I had been pulling in as an Actor, Writer, Whatever. After half an hour of bobbing and weaving, I gave
in. "Listen, you know me. You know I'm always going
to pull my own weight and be sure that we are okay
financially." (This is true. I am extremely debt averse.)
"But if I say I'm still bookkeeping or have a day job, I'll
still have one. If I say I won't, then I'm closer to not having one and just making a living as an artist."

He laughed. Not a mean laugh. A relieved laugh.
"Okay, Tony Robbins." He kept on hiking.

Right then and there I proclaimed myself semi-nuts
and stopped. All of it. I threw out all my notebooks,

read for pleasure on the subway, and never uttered another affirmation on the treadmill again. None of it made me happy. My life as an Actor, Writer, Whatever wasn't perfect. In fact, sometimes it was pretty damn hard. But it was what it was (and it is what it is) and it's fine. This power-of-attraction stuff wasn't me. I was forcing myself to behave contrary to my own nature. Before I started doing that stuff I would have calculated our incomes (a low estimate in order to be safely within our means), created a budget, and entered everything into a pristine spreadsheet. I like spreadsheets.

I'm not a leave-it-up-to-the-universe-er, and, actually, all my negative thinking has served me well. My fear of being penniless and destitute has made me live within my means, budget, and always have a little rainy-day fund (which is one of the reasons I can keep doing what I love, in spite of not making it big or having *Gelt HaMeforash*). I imagine the worst, but I prepare for those possibilities. If I have an audition I imagine the train delays (I leave early and am always on time). When I was the founder and producer of a small film festival, I anticipated every possible thing going wrong; the mic wouldn't work or the films' files would be damaged. I planned for every possible disaster. And when a few happened, I was prepared. Piece of cake.

And merrily I rolled along—until I heard a broadcast of the science-themed public radio show *Radio Lab* entitled "Deception." Former college competitive swimmer and now psychologist Joanna Starek wanted to ascertain what differentiated athletes who consistently outperformed from others with the same physiological capacity. She gave a "self-deception" questionnaire to a swim team and evaluated the results against the swimmers' performances at the end of the season. Time after time the swimmers who were self-deceivers, rating the highest in denying undesirable aspects of themselves, were the fastest swimmers and outshined the "realists." In fact, many new studies show that self-deceivers have better interpersonal skills, do better at business, and are just plain happier. Makes sense. I doubt Michael Jordan ever stepped on the court thinking, *We might lose today.*

I am so fucked.

quotable
encouragement

I ARRIVE AT the actors' studio to work as the reader for the night (that is, *an* actors' studio not *the* Actors' Studio—I'm not that fancy). "Readers" read the roles opposite the auditioning actors. Tonight is a faux audition: each actor has paid thirty-five dollars to perform for and chat briefly with a manager. If that seems like a racket, it is, but it's a necessary racket. Actors don't have the opportunity to sell their wares to industry contacts as they once did. In the days of yore, or of Carol Burnett, agents and casting directors would have open office hours or attend showcases on a regular basis. Now there are hundreds of showcases on any given night. Most of them are bad and, even worse, boring.

The embittering experience of restlessly shifting about in an uncomfortable chair while *not* being entertained, coupled with having to keep up with the vast amount of media out there today, keeps most agents and casting directors away. Besides, if you need to scope out new talent, why would you pay to see a mediocre showcase in a hole-in-the-wall black box with the intermingling scents of mold, stale beer, and body odor when *you* can get paid to have the talent come to you?

In the lobby, actors are readying themselves for their appointments. Some are applying makeup, fluffing their hair—primping as if it were their wedding day. Some practice while pacing back and forth—miming the action as they mouth the lines. It's like watching a contemporary Kabuki performance from another dimension. Others just sit there, quietly reading their scenes. I suspect these are the people who will do the best in the auditions.

I have to wait to be proven right. The manager I'm reading for is running a few minutes late. I pass the time by reading the Quotables in the waiting room. Quotables are those five-inch-by-five-inch cards containing quotes written in an offbeat font like HURCULANUM or Papyrus. Quotes like "Whether you think you can or think you can't, you're right" (Henry Ford) or "Go confidently in the direction of your dreams! Live the life you've imagined" (Thoreau). I read the Quotables and think, *Henry Ford fraternized with Nazis. Henry David Thoreau was a misanthropic drunk. These are not reliable sources.*

Of course, historical accuracy is not the point. The quotes are meant to encourage and inspire. They are small, laminated, and tastefully hung about, but still I feel as if they should be mounted on a dorm room wall or tacked to the inside of a sixteen-year-old's school locker. Sayings like this are not for cynics, pessimists, or even just realists. They are for people who believe they are special, who feel as though these quotes apply directly and deeply to them. They are for people whose optimism and self-esteem can shout over an occasional gnawing whisper of self-doubt. They are not for people who shout down even well-founded optimism. I mentally add my own Quotable to the lobby wall: "Actors endure long periods of unemployment, intense competition for roles, and frequent rejections in auditions" (U.S. Department of Labor, Bureau of Labor Statistics).

The manager arrives. The auditions start. A few of the actors are good—pull-back-the-curtain-and-ready-to-go-on-set good. Some are okay. Most are bad. And this should make me feel talented and fabulous by comparison, but it doesn't. It makes me feel dirty. Like the time I witnessed a homeless man, sitting on a subway bench in his own stench and filth, hitting himself in the head while chanting "Beast leave my body! Beast leave my body! Beast leave my body!" *I'm watching a deluded person at his most vulnerable*, I thought. It was intensely intimate and was an intimacy I did not earn or ask for. Except this time, at these auditions, I did.

The manager, of course, does not tell the bad actors that they did poorly. Among the lore of the Actor, Writer, Whatever is the tale of a manager/casting director/agent with a cigar firmly fixed to the side of his mouth, pointing a finger and barking, "You have no talent! You'll never make it in this town!" Then the Actor, Writer, Whatever goes on to become the biggest and brightest star in the universe. As per usual, the polar opposite is the case here. The manager says, "That was a great choice of material for you," and then follows up with some generic niceties that could be construed as compliments and don't seem very different from the notes he gives the actors who have had stellar auditions. All will leave feeling encouraged. "Hollywood is the only place in the world where you can die of encouragement" (Pauline Kael).

Only "beautiful" actors should take encouragement seriously. By beautiful, I mean *stunningly* beautiful. Very beautiful or even very *very* beautiful will not suffice. If people are falling all over themselves to get a look at you in Omaha or Peoria, forget it. You won't even get a second look in New York City or Los Angeles. You will be instantly downgraded to "attractive," or, even worse, "not unattractive." However, if you are a male or female in possession of extraordinary bone structure, perfectly symmetrical features, and a body without an ounce of fat, you are the exception. "It is better to be beautiful than to be good" (Oscar Wilde). Study with someone to get the bare minimum of skills, or get someone decent to coach you before auditions, and you are in good shape. You can be as dumb as a box of hair (in fact it's preferable) and you will work. Often. Most likely for forty-nine thousand dollars a week on a CBS primetime show solving crimes with Sherlockian intellectual agility while wearing a black cocktail dress, lab coat, and six-inch Pucci stilettos. It's a short shelf life, but ah what a lovely shelf. The rest of us have the shelf life of a Pop Tart. On the one hand, long. On the other hand, it's a Pop Tart.

I regard the good actors at the faux audition. Some of these competent auditioners will never get the right breaks and will eventually quit, the rigors of the industry and the lifestyle having become too much. This is a shame, because a lot of real talent is lost here. Some will move on to tangentially related careers like casting or management. Many will become yoga instructors. Still others, like me, will just keep plugging along, having a day job while Acting, Writing, Whatever-ing remains a condition of their lives, like managing diabetes or another incurable disease that requires constant care and attention.

The outcome for those who fell short in the audition is exactly the same. At one time in my career I would have given an audition as bad as the worst of the worst. I am certain of it. I just kept (and oh, how I *hate* this phrase) working on my craft. I still do. I never shake the feeling that I should be so much better. I always feel that I am missing the mark. "I am no artist—please come help me" (Michelangelo to his assistant). Encouragement, even when it goes beyond the generic "thanks, that was great," is never absorbed into my psyche. Perhaps that's also the difference between Actor, Writer, Whatevers who start out shitty (and most start out shitty) and grow, and those who start out good and never do.

The other day I Googled the hotshot of my college theater department. The drama professors loved him. He got the lead in every play. Everyone on campus thought he was destined for superstardom. I loathed him. He was arrogant and mean. Whether in class or in the dining hall, he was always onstage. The world was his reality show. Today, he doesn't have a single credit on the Internet Movie Database. I found his website—on his resume the most impressive credits were ensemble chorus roles at regional theaters. Sure, those are credits to be proud of, but not quite what our college selves imagined for the future. We, and he, were sure his name would be bright in Broadway lights.

I infer that he rested on his laurels. The encouragement at an early stage clearly did him no good. "The great majority of men are bundles of beginnings" (Ralph Waldo Emerson). Self-loathing and insecurity in good measure, though pesky passengers, are driving forces that propel Actor, Writer, Whatevers beyond the bundle of beginnings.

This seems to be a condition that success and celebrity can't cure. "My one regret in life is that I am not someone else" (Woody Allen). "Oh, damn! Here we go again! What were they thinking? They gave me this role; don't they know I'm faking it?" (Renée Zellweger). "I still think people will find out that I'm really not very talented. I'm really not very good. It's all been a big sham" (Michelle Pfeiffer).

Talented people who have "made it" think of themselves as lucky. Lucky people think of themselves as talented. Put that on a five-by-five card and laminate it.

| notes

THE OTHER MORNING, my friend Maggie called me for what Actor, Writer, Whatevers refer to as "notes."

"Mel, I'm editing my reel. It's too long. Do you have a minute?" I did. She emailed the video. I watched it. It was good, but she was right.

"It is too long. What did you want to cut?"

I agreed with all of her ideas, and added one of my own: "If you're going to fade out and then fade back in, you don't need the 'later' card," I told her.

"You think the fading out and in is enough?"

"Definitely."

We talked a bit more. I added that I would not cut a particular close-up. She looked absolutely luminescent (look at your favorite movie stars—not everyone takes a nice close-up). And those were the only notes I gave. My only agenda was to help a respected peer put her best foot forward. It felt good to be engaged, involved, and working toward a mutual goal.

Usually, though, I don't relish giving notes. "Constructive criticism" is an oxymoron. Criticism is, by its very nature, deconstructive. As with most skills, some people are highly proficient at it and some are on the highly deficient end of the spectrum.

I fall somewhere in the middle. I do make sure I've checked my ego at the door and my only motivation is to make the work the best it can be. (How many Actor, Writer, Whatevers does it take to change a lightbulb? Only one. But the rest will say they could have done it better.) I try to be sensitive to the recipient's feelings, never give unsolicited notes, and be as specific as possible. Sometimes I lack the skill to concisely articulate a feeling that something in the work is a bit off. When I can't be specific or helpful, I shut up.

I seek the same in notes on my own writing. Sometimes they sting, but there's a real benefit to fresh eyes from a trusted source. One of my trusted sources works as a script doctor and was a Sundance-winning director. When his notes arrive in my inbox I greet them with both excitement and trepidation. He usually points out something painfully accurate that sends me back to the drawing board with hours of rewrites, but in the end I'm grateful for the illumination: a painful relief, like having stitches removed. Sometimes I'm too safe with my characters. He saves me from that.

Another trusted source is my acting coach. He's been in the business for over twenty years and is one of the most respected acting coaches in the country. One time, after watching an actress do a beautiful take of a scene from my script, he turned to me and said, "See how you've let yourself out of that one a little too easily. You should up the stakes here." He was right. I was being precious. I had given in to my personal propensity to avoid drama just where I needed to heighten it. I made the rewrites.

I trust these people not only because of their integrity and ability, but also because they see me as a colleague and an artist, and treat me as a professional. (In spite of never having sold anything, I am a professional. No, really, I am.) Their notes are pointed and smart and not at all vague, leaving me energized to roll up my sleeves and get back to work.

I'm this particular about whom I ask for notes because Acting, Writing, Whatever-ing is deeply personal work and it takes a while to learn what criticism to take with that proverbial grain of salt—what to wash down and what to let wash over you. Criticism is tough and a tough thing to gauge for yourself. We've all heard the story of focus groups panning a film that went on to be a smash hit. Then again, we've also heard the story of the director with final cut approval who disregards the studio and focus groups and goes on to have an unmitigated bomb. Notes are tricky that way. That's why I seek out professionals whom I respect, who lack ulterior motives, to give me feedback.

But alas, still I get notes from unwanted sources. After which I am not energized to roll up my sleeves and get back to work. Instead, I feel violated. Like I am being used to elevate the critiquer's sense of self. At best, they get to feel smart and helpful. At worst, a hierarchy is established in which I am not the alpha.

Once I invited a friend—we'll call him Ashok— to take a look at my screenplay and attend a reading. Though I do really like him, I have given him the name "Ashok" because I think it's a bit . . . unfortunate. The protagonist of my screenplay was a computer programmer. Ashok was a computer programmer. I had done my research. I thought computer language was accurate, but I asked him for confirmation. I didn't want his opinion regarding the creative components.

I got an email a few days after I sent him the script.

Page four. Three drinks. Not enough.

Apparently Ashok had taken it upon himself to give me notes, rather than answer my simple question: *Are the three sentences of programming language accurate? Yes or no?*

It got worse when he came to the reading. The actors were wonderful, as I knew they would be. They provided me with useful notes. I disagreed with a few but agreed with most. One actor in particular had a great insight regarding a supporting character's bit of dialogue. It wasn't huge, but it made a difference in that character's arc and I was grateful for it. All in all, the script was well received. Everyone hated the title, which has since changed.

After partaking in my post-discussion spread (Actor, Writer, Whatever rule number one: if people do something nice for you like participate in your screenplay reading, feed them often and well), everyone filed out except for Ashok, who then said, "Do you want to talk about this now?"

"Eh . . . sure."

He lay out on my couch like a Hollywood exec from another era. I half expected "the girl" to come in and start feeding him grapes. He went page by page by page. Three drinks weren't enough to get the protagonist drunk. Being a single guy, he would have an expensive sound system in addition to a fancy TV. He went on for half an hour.

Finally, I interrupted him. "But the programming lingo was accurate?"

"Yes. It's accurate."

"Thanks." I wanted to strangle him.

This may sound elitist, but I do not appreciate notes from people who have not made drama their vocation. Experienced actors, writers, directors, and sometimes even producers understand the art of storytelling, and thus have the qualifications to deconstruct a script. Being an avid moviegoer does not make you an expert. I may have a habit of sitting on my couch, screaming at the TV, "Bench this guy! Bring in the closer!" but I assume that Joe Girardi would not seek my counsel or welcome my "notes."

Another time, my husband came home all abuzz with enthusiasm. "Joan is going to help you."

"Who? Joan our neighbor?"

"Yes. Joan our neighbor."

The story: He ran into her on the street. They started talking. I have no idea how it came up that I was an actor and a writer. Joan's daughter had been a child star, and now, at the tender age of twenty-eight, was a producer. She would try to help me. Help me . . . how?

I'm not sure. What was this semi-retired CPA going to do, exactly? And I had never heard of her daughter . . . but no one's ever heard of me either, so hey, who knows?

The next time I ran into Joan, it was weird. "Sean told me he had a long talk with you," I said. "I didn't know you were involved in the entertainment industry."

"Not me. My daughter." Smiles all around. Awkward pause.

"Well . . ." More smiles. More awkwardness. "Okay, well, I should get going."

That night I told my husband of the encounter. "That's strange," he said.

"Wasn't it?"

The next time I saw Joan, I commented on how beautiful her Japanese maple was. I asked about her son's luck in finding a job after graduating college. I avoided the topic of The Business like a flesh-eating disease, but she brought it up. "Do you ever let people read your screenplays?"

"Sure." And I do. If they're not being produced, *somebody* should enjoy them. Maybe she'd enjoy them and I'd get the pleasure of having entertained someone. Maybe she'd hook me up with her daughter and we'd enjoy working together. Who knows? I took her email address.

A few weeks went by. My husband came home and told me he ran into Joan that morning. "She said that she liked them. She said she's going to put her thoughts together and send you an email."

"Our semi-retired CPA neighbor is going to give me *notes*?"

"I guess. Does that make you cringe a little?"
"Yep."

And it arrived in my inbox. On, of all things, a Sunday night. (Sunday nights already feel icky, due to the dreaded Monday mornings.) For a semi-retired CPA, she certainly had the entertainment industry development assistant critique sandwich down pat: Praise praise praise praise praise praise praise. Criticism criticism. Praise.

Hi Mellini,

Thanks for letting me read your screenplays! Your writing is really good, I think. You are able to create characters and scenes that are interesing, colorful, believable, funny. The story narratives flow well. Dialogue feels natural. The only criticism/suggestion that I have to offer is that *Enlightened in New Jersey*'s denouement may be a bit protracted. I wonder if there is a way to resolve something(s) earlier—perhaps the conflict with the mother?— and then wrap up the ending more quickly.

I really enjoyed reading both scripts. Good luck with this work. You've got a lot of talent!

Best,

Joan

I typed a reply.

Dear Joan,

Thank you so much for your critique of my screenplays. I thought you were asking to read them (it was you that asked to read them not the other way around) out of curiosity, enjoyment, or even perhaps to mine for an opportunity for your daughter . . . but getting unsolicited writing advice from a semi-retired CPA is so much better! Thank you! I am a dilettante and a neophyte and don't find your praise of my talents at all patronizing. I love it. I will be sure to disregard my friend the Sundance-winning director and professional script doctor. I spit on the contradictory opinion of my award-winning theater director/coach with over twenty years of experience in the industry. I made a big mistake seeking advice from industry peers instead of you, as you are so much more qualified to criticize me, my semi-retired CPA neighbor.

I feel bad. I feel guilty. How can I repay you? I really feel your generosity deserves a quid pro quo. How 'bout I come to your workplace and critique you there? No. That doesn't feel right. That's hardly on par with this lovely feeling you've given me. I know, how 'bout I meet your children and write up a little critique sandwich on your parenting skills . . . your life's work, so to speak. I will try to keep my notes from being too protracted. Praise praise praise praise praise praise praise. Criticism criticism. Praise.

All My Best,

Mellini

PS. You misspelled *interesting*.

My finger hovered over the key but I didn't hit *send*. I opened myself up to this (actually, my husband opened me up to this). What did I expect? Of course she was going to share her opinions. Guarding my work from unwanted notes was my responsibility.

The problem with giving civilians my work is that they forget or don't realize that no one likes unsolicited criticism about anything, ever. After my boundaries have been stomped over, I then feel obligated to be gracious, not point out that I didn't ask for an opinion (when oh, dear god, I really want to), and save the critiquer's feelings—like when someone spills red wine on your white couch. *No no no, it's okay. It will come right out (probably).*

I deleted my email and wrote:

Thanks, Joan.

Before I hit *send*, I thought better of it. I didn't want to be mis-e-terpreted as passive-aggressive or snarky.

Thanks, Joan!

I hit *send*. And hate myself.

Again (and again and again), I'm not universally opposed to notes. And if you hire me to write something, I will not be protective of it. Writers are hired guns. *So the protagonist is now from Mars? No problem.* Away I will type. But while a project still belongs to me, the only notes I want are the ones I ask for.

My worst unwelcome-notes incident happened at a filmmakers' networking event. The Business is a business of relationships, and I didn't have many. I was proud of forcing myself to get out from behind my laptop and meet people, forgetting that nothing good happens on a day that you burn the skin off your lip. Okay, so it wasn't burnt off. More like violently ripped off.

Apparently it is not wise to use retinol products prior to waxing. I did not know this. I shed many tears and lost swaths of my epidermis—not just on my lip but on my forehead as well. My hairline ends where my eyebrows begin. I also wax my sideburns, except on Halloween, when I wear purple and call myself Prince. Hair grows everywhere on me. It's a constant battle and one of those things that gives my ego a little jab every day when I look in the mirror. In addition, I notice the gaps between my canines and incisors. I also went to state college.

But I digress.

This may be why I have no personal velocity. I do not come across as someone who is good at what she does, in spite of (and this might sound both cocky and self-contradicting) having talent. The rest of it I am simply horrible at. This is why I still have a day job.

I showed up at this networking event trying not to feel self-conscious about my lip (thankfully, my bangs hid the forehead fiasco). I had a glass of wine. I greeted my friend Kim, a documentary filmmaker. I talked to a soap actor whom I had met a couple of days before. He was the new heartthrob who replaced the old heart-throb. I was the nurse who helped move the patient from the gurney to the operating table. After I got my script, I called the casting director. She had told me it was an under-five role but I had no lines. Although zero lines is literally under five lines, I thought there had been a mix-up. There was no mix-up. I was an under-five with no lines. Apparently, per union rules, when you and three other people move someone from a gurney to an operating table, it is considered an under-five role because there's a rehearsal involved. I did not tell friends and family the airdate.

Again, I digress.

After a few glasses of wine I started talking to a semi-hipster-type young woman. For the purposes of this story I am going to call her Bertha. No offense to the Berthas of the world; it just gives me pleasure to give her a name that makes "Ashok" sound melodious (only those with absolutely no power in the universe in which they operate resort to such pettiness).

Our conversation was pleasant enough. Bertha was an independent director who worked for MTV, or something like that. I told her my plight: I had a script. A good script. I was looking for "names to attach" (actors with easily recognizable names to commit to the project), because I'd heard that's what you do when you have a script, though I had absolutely no idea whatsoever what to do once I had the name attached.

Anyway, she said her ex (ex-boyfriend? husband? wife? boss?) might have ideas and she'd be happy to look at the script, et cetera. She seemed genuinely enthusiastic and eager to help. I emailed it to her the next day.

Then I sent follow-up emails over the next few months, like the good little networker I was trying to be. I always received an apologetic reply. So sorry, she hadn't read the script yet but she was definitely going to get to it in the next day or two.

Instead I received an emailed video of a "short film" she made. She said she was proud of it and wanted to share it—with, given the mass email, apparently everyone she knew. I watched it. It was a *Secret*-like advertisement for some sort of self-help New Age-y type guru. I email a reply:

Looks great!

And it did look great. A self-help infomercial with a live jazz ensemble accompanying the host in a manner that would make Kerouac roll way the fuck over in his grave—it was not at all cheesy. Of course, I'm being sarcastic (sarcasm is the humor of the weak): it should have been served over stale nachos at a sports arena. I sent back a supportive response because it was the polite thing to do.

I wasn't being totally disingenuous. If I kept in mind that the purpose of the video was to sell whatever this self-help guru cum beat poet was selling, she had met her goal. The production quality was not bad . . . but I got a sinking feeling in my gut. *This person may not be the player she presented herself to be.* Perhaps giving her my script was a bad idea. I went to her website and viewed her other clips. They were all pseudo hip-hoppy promos, which is great if your client is in fact MTV, but Bertha's clips did not share my . . . aesthetic sensibility. It was as if I was asking Sylvester Stallone to help out on a Jim Jarmusch project.

But hope springs eternal. One sad part of being an Actor, Writer, Whatever is the daydreams. I talk myself down from them, but initially I can't help but go there. Every time I go on a commercial audition, my imaginings take me beyond the callback, beyond booking and filming the job, to the paycheck and residuals, which are cashed and in my bank account accruing interest (at a very favorable rate). Every time someone reads my script I envision a fortuitous chain of events that eventually results in owning a co-op (even in my fantasy, my co-op is still just a modest postwar 800-square-foot, two-bedroom, fourth-floor walk-up) and being interviewed by Terry Gross or Charlie Rose. I would join the ranks of the stars who gush over them. *Oh, Charlie/Terry, I've been such a big fan for so long and this has really truly been my pleasure.* They really are the best.

But again, I digress.

I knew I'd been clear about just wanting advice on attaching name actors, but I couldn't shake the feeling that I'd made myself vulnerable in a way that I did not wish to be with this person I barely knew. There was a discord between the way Bertha presented herself— or, perhaps more fairly, the way I interpreted her—and what her work was. Still, the fantasy side of my brain was not cooperative in processing this logic. I wanted to believe that maybe she had this promo-making New Age-y thing as a day job . . . that she really wanted to produce independent films and we'd go on to produce my film and have this wonderful long-term filmmaking collaboration together. This "ex" of hers was an agent or the like, with a cache of name stars who were actively looking for indie projects. I sent her another email.

Are you coming to the next networking night?

She replied.

Yes, and I promise I'll read your screenplay by then!

I had no idea why she used an exclamation point and no idea what to expect. I watched my fabulous fantasy scenarios dissolve to black. I felt queasy.

I showed up at the bar on the Bowery. Bertha was at the bar chatting with another semi-hipster-type woman. Poised in her hand was a glass of wine so large I was surprised not to see a goldfish doing backflips in it. I had barely taken a step inside when she spoke—not "hello," not "how are you," not any sort of generic pleasantry whatsoever. Her first words of greeting were "So, do you want to talk about your script?" I knew I didn't. I really didn't.

"Sure. I'm going to get a drink first." I'm no fool. I needed a drink for what was coming. The critique sandwich. It was clear she was the sort who was not going to let her expertise go to waste. She was going to have to let me know she was the alpha. You can't be an alpha without an underling: me. Hooray.

I returned with my own goldfish bowl of chardonnay. She pointed to a booth in the corner. "Shall we go over there and talk?" Her voice held more graveness than my mother-in-law's when she called to tell us that our beloved grandmother would not make it through the night. I prepared myself for the critique sandwich. Braced and ready—bring it on, lady. Supersize me.

My butt barely met the seat before she said, "You have the same problem that I sometimes have. Your story doesn't have a beginning, middle, and end."

What the fuck?

Obviously, Bertha was not aware of the appropriate protocol for slamming someone. Even if you want to be the alpha of all you survey, you must do the critique sandwich. When you don't it's like taking a massive dump at an intimate dinner party and not flushing before leaving the loo.

"What?" was all I could muster in reply. Always the Actor, Writer, Whatever, I made a quick mental note that people usually say "what?" because they are processing what the other person is saying. Not because they didn't hear. And I couldn't believe what I was hearing. I know what my work is and what it isn't. And I know without a doubt that my stories always always always have an undeniable arc. There is always a distinctive beginning, middle, and end. This was going to be bullshit.

She could have said something closer to my proclivities; she could have said that I needed more tension in the second act; she could have said I needed to make the stakes higher for the protagonist; she even could have said I needed more backstory. (I'm a big believer in minimal backstory. I respect my audience and strive to ignite their imaginations. Incidentally, the more commercial the film, the more backstory you get.) If she had said any of the above I would have paid her due respect, even if she hated it. This was going to be painful.

She went on. "What you have here is a good character study. This would be a good short, but not a feature film."

Are you motherfucking kidding me?

It didn't stop there. She went on for what felt like forever with this, that, and the other thing . . . all of which seemed to have nothing to do with my script and a lot more to do with showing off that she could deconstruct with the baddest of badass English majors.

I said nothing. Close to nothing. I did point out that she was correct in her assessment that a piece of dialogue made no sense for character A, but it was actually character B who had said it, so . . . ?

At long last, she mercifully concluded her lecture. "I wrote more detailed notes in the margins for when you want to review them."

"Thanks."

I accepted the script back. I didn't want her notes. Her notes were shit. I wanted the paper. I can't edit on the computer. I have to edit on paper with a pen in hand but have enviro-guilt about killing trees, so after a revision I flip the paper over and print the next draft on the reverse side. Bertha had printed my emailed script, so this was guilt-free gratis paper. I also wanted the binder clip. Binder clips, paper: all these costs add up.

Initially, I felt good about keeping my piehole shut and patiently letting the criticism pass. How would it have served me to get defensive? It would have made me even more her underling. My thought was, *This is who you need to be, and I am going to be gracious enough to let you.* And, oddly, it felt good . . . well, *mostly* good. There is most certainly something ennobling about turning the other cheek. And there is most certainly something humiliating about turning the other cheek.

Later that night, I told the story to my husband.

"Did that make you cringe?"

"Yes," I said, "it made me cringe." I would have said more, but he had already fallen asleep. I crawled out of bed, slipped into my desk chair, and opened up the script. In the margins were her notes written in bubbly girl handwriting—I half expected the *i*'s to have little hearts over them.

Page 67:

Interesting parallel but more effectively conveyed by showing rather than explain. Spend some time sketching between the two worlds. Judy=Wanda. Hanuma=Boss etc.

And, before I was even aware of it, I started writing a rebuttal.

I would hardly call a one-line parenthetical on page 67 overly expository. It's one line. On page 67. If my screenplay is a "character study," as you say, and a "piece of crap," as you imply, why did you wait until page 67 to start writing your opus in the margins? By the way, the proper grammatical construction is "showing" and "explaining."

Page 67:

> GURU
>
> I knew there was something special about
>
> you.

Really? Why? We never see what makes Shantanu special.

Maybe you should have read the first sixty-six pages. Just a thought. Reading sometimes helps me understand things, but that's just me.

Page 72:

Are you playing these scenes/characters for comedy or sincerity? Tone waivers between both. The "marmalade" works as a punchline. But embedded here w/in this speech, defangs it, feels inconsistent.

I wrote this script to have a real emotional life, but in comic timing. You're right. It is inconsistent, but since every film from Howard Hawks's 1939 classic Only Angels Have Wings *to* When Harry Met Sally *to* Bridesmaids *has done the same, I thought I could too.*

Page 75:

Why this sudden change of tone?

Because the characters are arguing and sometimes when people argue, their tone changes. Sorry if this was confusing.

Page 76:

When did he realize this?

See pages 1–75.

Page 86:

                    Meenakshi

        No I'm not. I'm the anti-mom. I swear like
        a sailor ...

Interesting character traits that should be seen throughout the film not told about near the end.

Okay. This strips you of any benefit of doubt and confirms that you are shredding my work apart to feel like a big person. I went back and checked EVERY LINE of this character's dialogue. She swears in EVERY LINE. As in, EVERY LINE.

Page 91:

                    Shantanu

    Woe. Wow.

Whoa

This is the only useful note you've given me. The correct slang spelling is indeed "whoa."

Page 92:

                    Nancy

    I know. But you'll be happy to know
    I decided to finish. I start a program
    in the fall. So in about three years
    I'll be PhD granny.

An issue we've never heard about before?

Except at the end of act one, when there's a huge family blowup and Shantanu insults his mother about never finishing her dissertation. You know, that HUGE scene at the end of act one. The one that's pivotal to the plot of the whole film. Those five pages must not have been in your copy.

Page 92:
Why is it important to either of them or their relationship?

Because moving on after the death of a loved one is the THEME OF THE ENTIRE MOVIE. I am now calling you the C word.

I write all this and I feel better. And then I feel worse and petty and small . . . an underling. I flip the script over to the reverse side, place it in the printer tray, and go to bed.

to the author of
the secret

Dear Rhonda Byrne,

I am writing this letter to respectfully request a refund for your book, which I purchased at the Park Slope Barnes & Noble in Brooklyn. The store refused to take the book back, claiming I had clearly read it. Sure, I may have dog-eared a couple of pages while giving the text the most cursory of glances. Sure, this may have occurred during a nice soak in a hot bath with Epsom salts, but that should be inconsequential.

The reason? I had implicitly followed the book's instructions. I *visualized* the person behind the counter accepting the book and joyfully handing over my cash (not store credit). Over and over, I visualized walking up to the customer service counter, where a handsome gentleman, who could only be described as a cross between Cary Grant and a young Ricky Martin, would eye the book suspiciously and then give me those elevator up-and-down eyes. He'd try to hide his intrigue behind that veil of bookstore cashier professionalism, but in the end would be rendered powerless by the extraordinary creature standing in front of him (me). After a volley of amusing quips he would agree to give me the refund in exchange for my phone number. A wild romance would ensue.

This is not what came to pass, despite my crystalline projections. He refused to return my money, accusing me of dropping the book in a bathtub or something. He was also not a cross between Cary Grant and Ricky Martin. He was one of those doughy, pimply teenagers who are trilingual in English, Klingon, and Na'vi. And wild romance did not ensue. The little shit said I was too old for him.

I demand this refund because I prodigiously employed all the techniques in *The Secret*, yet my life remains hopelessly the same. Actually, I've employed the techniques in several books over several years: *Creative Visualization. Live What You Think. Think What You Are. Live What You Creatively Visualize That You Think That You Are Living You Are.*

Yes, of course, I've done my affirmations daily. *Money comes to me freely and easily. I already have everything I want. I am Midas.* This yielded no result. Yes, of course, I took great pains to state all my desires in the present tense. Yes, of course, I know every thought has an electrical charge that surges out into the universe and then boomerangs back to shock my life into shape. I know what you are going to ask: In the nanosecond before I started chanting my affirmations, did I have the thought, *my life has sucked before*, or *motherfucker, I hope this works*? Only the most officiously technically minded could construe these flashes as past-tense thoughts whose electrical charge zapped away hours of affirmations . . . so don't even go there.

I also did "the list," as prescribed by your book. I wrote down everything I wanted, complete with drawings, graphs, and pictures I clipped from *Dwell* magazine in order to bring the life of which I was desirous into visual shape. Just like the guy featured in the DVD version of *The Secret* (oh, right, I need a refund for the DVD too), whenever I do a deep-cleansing uncluttering detoxifying total *feng shui* or have to move due to eviction, I inevitably come across one of these lists. But, unlike with the handsome gazillionaire in the DVD, nothing on my list has come to fruition.

Is he single?

My therapist has helped me understand that I went to (state) college, have half a head on my shoulders, and should have made different choices in books to obsessively insert into every nook and cranny of my life. She suggested that instead of spending hours creatively visualizing or drawing up maps of future-tense me (as if it were present-tense me), I should have been working on my résumé and increasing my sessions to eight times a week. I'm taking her advice with a grain of salt. She's a frumpy middle-aged therapist. I have no desire to ever be a doctor of psychology or middle-aged—so why would I take *her* advice? I want to be an international superstar with six hundred Facebook friends. This is why I am moving to Hollywood to join the Church of Scientology and marry a handsome closeted celebrity. If you could send the check by the end of the month, that would be super.

Thanks!

Sincerely,

Mellini Kantayya

the antisocial network

EVERYTHING DIES.

Nothing lasts forever.

All things, including you, me, the sun, and the stars, will one day come to an end.

Can't get around it, no matter how sunny your disposition or how rose-colored your glasses. That goes double for Actor, Writer, Whatevers. Everyone in the entertainment industry, from the seven-figured studio head to the low-budget indie film intern, will eventually be pounding the pavement for their next gig. Thus, the entertainment industry is built on relationships. Networking is vital to staying employed. And, because networking is so vital to staying employed, I am often unemployed.

I hate networking. I am bad at it. One reason is that I developed slight prosopagnosia, or face blindness, after a head injury a few years back. I'm in good company: the artist Chuck Close is prosopagnosic, as is the author and neurologist Oliver Sacks, though my condition is nowhere near as severe. Oliver Sacks can't even recognize his own reflection in a mirror. I can easily recognize everyone I met before the accident and everyone with whom I have more than an acquaintance relationship. However, I fail to distinguish about a third of acquaintances or new people I meet from those I have never met, particularly if I'm seeing them out of the usual context. What's frustrating is that I can't figure out the formula. I have no idea whose face will make an imprint and whose won't. Especially vexing is when it happens with African Americans. I see the look in their eyes. I know what they're thinking: *We all look alike, right? Is that it?* I know this is what they are thinking because it is what I think when I'm mistaken for another South Asian woman. I want so badly to say, "Hey, *all* people look alike to me—not just black people. An accident left me with prosopagnosia dagnabbit!" But I don't want to over-share. I'll bare my soul in my work but would rather be mistaken for a racist than over-share. Over-sharing with strangers or people you barely know is rarely appropriate . . . unless you're in a therapist's office or Northern California.

I am a bad networker also because of my hermit-like tendencies. I used to vacillate between party girl and hermit, but now it's mostly hermit. No more cocktails on weeknights, especially before a gig or audition. I can't process alcohol the way I used to and I wind up looking like a puffer fish the next day. I have a kid. My day job starts at five a.m. I need as much beauty sleep as possible to preserve what little I have left. (Insert Women Growing Older clichés here, e.g., "The industry's double standard is so unjust! Women in entertainment are expected to either stay young or stay home," or, "I didn't appreciate my twenty-year-old ass, and now I weep for it. I weep for it," or, "I've come full circle to appreciate fine lines and wrinkles because they're symbols of every step I've taken on my life's journey—they're laugh lines, not wrinkles, thank you very much!" Pretend I did the whole shtick and proceed directly to the obligatory sticking-finger-down-throat-while-rolling-eyes gesture.)

Also, I've never felt like I totally fit in with other Actor, Writer, Whatevers. On a TV or film set I often feel like a foreigner. I speak the language but I'm not sure I comprehend everything that's going on. I'm a little off. I don't mean when the cameras are rolling; I mean during the lunchtime small-talk chitchat at the craft service table. Actor, Writer, Whatevers are a tribe of people who didn't fit in elsewhere, yet it seems I was separated from my tribe and raised by wolves. Stumbling, awkward wolves.

But my friends, especially those with careers far removed from the arts, keep urging me to network. "Get out there. Meet people. Make connections!" Like I'm some sad new divorcée. I never know exactly what they mean. Do I attend networking events? Shake hands and pass my headshots out to everyone? Selling myself feels contrived and smarmy, even with people I know and like. My neighbor is a writer for a hit network sitcom. A friend's husband is a successful movie producer. What does parlaying those relationships into opportunities even look like? And how does one do so without feeling like an asshole? Yet many people can and do exactly that. They navigate these murky waters with ease and charm and never feel as if they need to shower afterward. I am not one of those people.

Facebook initially appeared to be the perfect elixir: I didn't have to go out to feel like a social klutz. I could feel like a social klutz at home and get a full eight hours of sleep. Having a name printed alongside a photo not only compensated for my slight prosopagnosia, but also vastly increased my chances of recognizing someone when I saw them again. I could post my upcoming gigs without feeling like a braggart.

It was great at first. I reached out to a television producer I had once met with a question about writing treatments. He posted great advice within an hour. A casting director posted her status as needing a reader for a casting session. I replied, and later that day I was reading opposite actors auditioning for a prime-time network drama. I posted an error message I kept getting when syncing my phone and laptop. A friend quickly posted the fix, saving the day and my data.

But it wasn't all fairy-tale endings in the Book of Face. Facebook can be an artist's worst enemy. It's the world's most perfect facilitator of procrastination. I'd hop on to check my newsfeed and then shake myself awake to realize I'd spent over an hour looking at pictures of friends' babies. I could have been doing something productive, like finishing the second act of my screenplay . . . or dusting something.

Facebook quickly negated one of the perks of moving to the big city: climbing out of the hometown pigeonhole. My New York friends didn't think of me as the girl who peed her pants in kindergarten and then tried to pass it off as spilt lemonade (*yes, I know I had milk in my lunchbox, but I also had lemonade, which I happened to spill in this perfect circle shape around the crotch of my pants*). So much for self-reinvention. Now, everyone from nursery school onward was friend-ing me, tagging me in embarrassing college photos, posting on my wall, "Remember that time you peed your pants in kindergarten and tried to pass it off as spilt lemonade? That was so funny!" There's a reason people fall out of touch.

I also started to feel like a public relations director for a presidential candidate, thinking and rethinking how each status post would play within each demographic of Facebook friend. How will this go over with my friends in the business? Friends at Burning Man? Friends who are born again? For example, take the word *douche*. I love the word *douche*, whether in the diminutive or the extended form *douchebag*. When you want to call someone a *douche*, nothing but *douche* will do. However, some do find *douche* objectionable. Go figure.

Then there were the curtains I just didn't need to look behind. For instance, I didn't want to know that my commercial agent spent working hours playing various Facebook games. I grew increasingly resentful of her racking up points on Bedazzled at ten o'clock on a Tuesday morning rather than procuring auditions for me. I also could have done without reading about her courtship with her boyfriend, then fiancé, and then every minuscule detail of her wedding planning from start to finish. She is no longer at the agency. Her Prince Charming swept her away somewhere. They live in a powder-blue colonial with their two cats, Smoochy and Pepper. I would be happy for her, but I liked her better when she was single, unhappy, not playing Bedazzled, and getting me auditions.

I lowered my opinion of other "friends" on Facebook. Like the Blurt Out Whatever Passes Through Your Head Guy. A director whom I was initially fond of posted:

> Why are so many grips fat? Doesn't all that lifting & carrying burn calories?

I liked him much less after that post. I wanted to comment:

> Grips work very long and hard. In my experience, they are often the most likable people on set, having the ability to stay calm and keep their senses of humor even when things get tense. Why insult them? Especially if they're doing you a favor by working under ultra–low–budget conditions for ultra–low wages on your stupid film about a Hassidic porn star's search for true love. If I were a grip I would sit on you to teach you a lesson.

I wanted to leave that comment, but of course I didn't.

The Indie Whiner wasn't much better. By most estimations, she would be considered a successful filmmaker—not Spielberg successful, but successful nonetheless. Yet all she posted were complaints about the business:

No one's funding quality work anymore.

And:

There's just no respect for artists in the studio system.

Or:

The distribution options for indie filmmakers suck.

Yes, these things are problems, but they are troubles to be shared with your friends at the bar, not on Facebook. I wanted to comment:

Your film got made. I saw it at my local theater. I can get it on Netflix. Please shut

the fuck up and kindly observe the more
fitting practice of counting lucky stars.
Many would gladly sacrifice their left booby
for your "problems." Whining in a public
forum makes you sound like, for lack of a
better word, a douche.

I wanted to leave that comment, but of course
I didn't.

However, I reached the pinnacle of my newfound
misanthropy with the Self-Promoting Indie Producer.
His statuses (stati? statum?) were self-promotion bor-
dering on self-adulation, under the pretense of crowd-
sourcing and sharing woes:

Ack! Combing through a list of 824
"industry" peeps at Sundance to choose
10 to meet with for the producing lab re:
"Stop Crying, Big Boy" directed by Becky
Kranberg—by five p.m. today! Whom
should I grace with my presence?

I was dumbstruck. Are we, your Facebook audience, really to believe you're exasperated and over-
whelmed and not just letting people know you got into
the Sundance producers' lab? I couldn't even think of a

single snarky comment to post on the imaginary Facebook in my head.

There's a saying among therapists, *don't judge your insides by other people's outsides.* When we feel insecure, awkward, and downright nuts, while everyone around us seems so self-possessed and together, it's unfair to compare our inner reality to another's outward presentation. But on Facebook people post their inner realities, hopes, dreams, fears, passing thoughts, and what they had for breakfast. Facebook gives me the illusion I'm glimpsing someone's insides, as if I'm reading their diary, one line, one day at a time. It gives me the same strange commingling feelings of superiority, disdain, affection, and interest I get when I watch reality TV. In essence, that's what Facebook is: a small-screen reality program where I've accepted or sought out the cast of players. Sometimes I'm a performer, sometimes I'm the audience, but there I am, scrolling through the newsfeed, half expecting this status:

Bargain-table author shuns Facebook over-sharing . . . in *memoir.* Yeeeesh.

why you frontin'

I NO LONGER have a recurring supporting role on a soap opera. The show, the last soap opera left shooting in New York City, was canceled. I will miss employment. "I have a recurring supporting role on a soap opera" sounds infinitely better than "I am an actor who has not had a paying gig in seven months, three weeks, and six days. Oh, and I'm a screenwriter too . . . though nothing's ever been produced. Excuse me . . . bartender? Another white wine spritzer, and keep 'em comin'."

I will also miss chatting with the very sweet and funny casting director. I'll miss the makeup guy who made me look fabulous, the woman in the hair department with great toddler-wrangling tips, the gruff yet lovable stage managers . . . people who, like me, will soon be unemployed. What I will not miss is the schlep to pick up my script.

After casting books me, they leave my script at the security desk. Thankfully, it's a twenty-four-hour security desk. Between the kid and the day job, the most convenient time for me to make the fifty-five-minute trek from Brooklyn to the Upper (then-walk-way-the-hell) West Side is at night. One evening, amid a particularly hectic and exhausting week, I ventured out without my usual spackling of makeup, wearing . . . sweatpants. This may not seem like a big deal in other parts of the country, but on the island of Manhattan, it's the equivalent of wearing your bathrobe to a business meeting. Here, every week is Fashion Week. Whether it's West Village chic or Lower East Side hip, everyone's got a put-together look. But I figured the odds were in my favor. In a city of over eight million people, what were the chances I'd run into someone I knew?

Apparently, good. Waiting on the subway platform to return home, I looked up to see Rodney. Rodney had appeared in the first play I wrote and directed Way-Off-Broadway. He and another guy were sporting their hipster finest, clearly setting sail toward the adventures of a New York Monday night. I felt naked. Worse than naked. I felt sweatpants. I buried my head in my script, hoping he wouldn't notice me.

"Mellini?" *Damn.*

"Hey, Rodney, I didn't see you there." We did the customary half hug with a kiss to the air on the left of the cheek.

"This is my friend John."

"Hey, John." Shake hands.

"John and I just finished an indie that I directed and produced. John wrote and starred in it."

"Wow. That's great."

"Yeah. Thanks. We're waiting to hear from Sundance."

"Wow. That's great."

"We're a shoo-in for a lot of other festivals, but obviously we want to premiere at Sundance. I'm pretty sure we will."

"Wow. That's great."

He regarded the script in my hand. "What's that?"

"Oh, uh . . . I have a teeny little role on a soap every now and again." Hundreds of headshots and résumés land on the casting director's desk each month. Of the people who are selected to audition, fewer than 5 percent land a day-player or under-five role. Of those actors, even fewer get a recurring appearance, never mind one that has spanned more than six years. I should feel proud. Yet when asked, I always feel the need to qualify it. I downplay not so much to be modest, but to remind

myself, *Don't get too proud, Little Miss Icarus. It can
all melt away and you'll go plummeting back to the ter-
restrial sphere.*

"A soap?" Rodney replied. "I didn't think they
made those anymore."

"Lucky for me, they do." (Crazy foreshadowing,
right?) "Well, here's the train. Great seeing you."

I boarded a different car on the train. I didn't want
to hear any more of Rodney's résumé. When I last saw
Rodney, I was in the final stages of adopting my daughter, and had since become a mother. He didn't ask about
this, nor did I expect him to. For some Actor, Writer,
Whatevers the only news worth hearing or sharing is
on your résumé.

I wonder if Rodney's résumé isn't a little padded.

I remember Rodney "frontin' "* since way back
when. Even with extra work, he'd blow it up to be the
greatest gig ever. He'd brag about having the cast and
crew in stitches, how the director loved him so much
he vowed to put him in all his films, how he was going
to hook up with the lead actress. When he was a production assistant he would talk about how the company
was going to fund his short film. Most of these boasts

---

* frontin' *verb* \'frən-tin\ To behave or to present oneself in an inauthentic manner with the intention of misleading or impressing others (e.g., *Joe frontin' like
he all that, but he has no job and lives in his mama's basement*).

did not come to pass. But every now and then, something would. And then something else would. Then he
built on that momentum. And then he had himself a
career. Obviously someone was buying the fish (story)
Rodney was selling.

Rodney is a player. Rodney is a hustler. I say this
with both disdain and jealousy. Jealousy because Rodney was able to front himself right into a decent career,
something I have not managed to do. Disdain because I
don't think Rodney is all that talented.

But who am I to judge? And why not talk
yourself up? The whole entertainment industry is
built on reinvention, illusion, and fantasy, is it not?
Acting, Writing, Whatever-ing is playing make-believe
for money. PR and marketing are basically frontin'
with a high-gloss veneer. It would behoove me to do
a little frontin' myself. But, sadly, whenever I front it
comes off as conspicuously affected and over-eager.
Like the way my mother acted on my seventh birthday as I unwrapped not a toy or a book, but hand-sewn
pajamas from my aunt Ernestine. "Look at those lovely
pajamas! Just adorable! You were just saying that you
wanted some cute pajamas, and those are sure something else!"

Can't blame Mom. I have a hard time selling "me"
as a product, and I'm certainly more desirable than

pajamas on a seven-year-old's birthday. I find it impossible to even motivate myself to sell myself. It takes effort. Effort I'd rather spend on something worthwhile. . . like watching television. If I wanted to go into sales I would have gone with a profit-making product like guns or benzodiazepines (Xanax).

Besides, I haven't reached my ten thousand hours yet.

In his book *Outliers*, Malcolm Gladwell proposes that it takes ten thousand hours to achieve mastery in just about any field. Be it math, music, sports, or even crime, practice really does make perfect. By my estimations I will reach my ten thousand hours of Acting, Writing, Whatever-ing in about 3.604 years. What shall I do with my newfound expertise? I will not have put a dent in the number of hours it would take to perfect the art of self-promotion. I will be masterful in the work, but not in bringing my work to the marketplace. My post-ten-thousand-hour masterworks will keep company with my pre-ten-thousand scripts: unproduced on a shelf.

It's cold comfort that I am not alone in living this conundrum. In a perfect world all committed artists would have someone toiling behind the scenes, selling us so we could concentrate on our work. Even if there were more hours in the day and enough time for both work and PR, few artists would be inclined to split their attention. Most who are truly passionate about their work are passionate about *their work*. Frontin' just feels like an interloper in the love affair.

Lesser work can be accepted as better work simply because someone is better at packaging it. I find this more disheartening as a consumer of art than as a maker of it. I can't help but wonder what films I could be watching, books I could be reading, music I could be listening to. It makes me sad to think of what I'm missing . . . and a little sad to think of what the Rodneys of the world are missing too. There's something deeply satisfying in striving to be your personal best.

I still wish I had thrown on a t-shirt and jeans before I ran into him.

But what's done is done. I decided to take advantage of the elastic waistband feature on the sweatpants. I dashed out of the subway station and straight for the new ice cream shop in my neighborhood. This isn't ordinary ice cream—this is small batch, little bit of heaven, best ice cream you've ever had ice cream. The owner used to sell it out of a pushcart on the street. I was hooked at first taste, but despite Googling their website (still under construction), signing up for their email newsletter (never got one), and friend-ing them on Facebook (rarely posted anything), I didn't know a brick and mortar store was opening until I walked by it. I finally encountered someone worse at promotion than I was, but he was an ice cream genius. I was turning over which flavor of his brilliance I was going to enjoy when I arrived at the store. Closed. A handwritten sign was posted on the door: "We're sorry, we sold more than expected our opening weekend. We are going to regroup, make more ice cream, and open in a few days (with additional seating too!). We are touched by the support of the neighborhood. Thank you."

The store had to close three days after they opened their doors. They were miserable at marketing (I was actively seeking them out and I *still* couldn't find them), but they went through more than one hundred and twenty-five gallons of ice cream in three days. Every now and then, being good is good enough to get you noticed. A lesson I would have never learned if I wasn't wearing sweatpants.

the incredibly sticky, uncomfortable, complicated, minefield-laden subject of race

IT SEEMS the only white people who aren't even the teensy-eensiest bit uncomfortable with the subject of race are actual racist people. Ask a Klansman a question about race relations (go ahead, I'll wait) and he'll be chomping at the bit to share his "wisdom," off and running without the slightest hesitation. The moderately bigoted and the clueless will tie for second place. Lagging far behind will be the broad-minded non-racist white person. Ask this person about, say, institutional racism in a post-Obama age and they will pause, take a deep breath, and think very carefully before answering. After that, they will take another deep breath and then qualify their answer. Reasonable people know it's complicated, too vast and unruly to get a handle on. It's not any simpler for people of color and is even more knotted for those of us in entertainment.

I knew "making it," or even just making my way through this business, wasn't going to be easy. After all, I was in junior high before I saw a South Asian person on television. It was on a *CBS Schoolbreak Special* in an episode entitled "The Exchange Student." A teenage girl from India comes to live with an American teen and her family. The Indian exchange student is conservative, demure, and wears a sari. The American sister is a rocker (at least a tamer afterschool-special version of a rocker) and plays keyboards in a band. The American teen pulls the Indian teen into her rockin' world, expecting her to relish dressing and behaving like a rockin' American teen (the tamer afterschool-special version), causing the Indian teen to feel out of place and awkward. She clings to her traditional culture all the more. (Even in junior high the scenario rang false to me. When you take a teen from a strict conservative environment—traditional Indian, Catholic, born again—and put her into a permissive one, the story usually ends in a trip to the free clinic or a stomach pump.) The American teen is frustrated the Indian teen won't conform. The Indian teen is hurt the American teen won't accept her for who she is.

This conflict's crescendo comes at the top of the third act, with an earnest-yet-dramatic *Dawson's Creek*–style confrontation, which begins with an awareness and articulation of emotions atypical of real teens and ends with the more typical stomping off and slamming of doors. *Will the two "sisters" ever be friends again?*

The intricacies of this plot are resolved at the Camp David of TV teens—the Big School Dance. The American teen's band performs, and she dedicates a song she wrote to her Indian "sister." She sings about the beauty of their differences and how much she's learned. The sari-clad exchange student is so moved she breaks out into a dance, which we take to be traditionally Indian, though it more closely resembles the dance from the "Walk Like an Egyptian" video or Steve Martin's King Tut impersonation.

This is not what I had in mind when I moved to New York. I did not want to wear a sari and do a walk-like-an-Egyptian-Steve-Martin-impersonation-of-King-Tut-type dance while my host sister belted a power ballad jamming out on the keyboards. I wanted to be Maddie in *Moonlighting*. I wanted to do edgy, quirky indie films. I wanted to be Jane Russell in a remake of *Gentlemen Prefer Blondes*. I just wanted to do my thing like any other Actor, Writer, Whatever. I didn't want the responsibility of breaking down barriers. I am too easily distracted and lazy for that sort of thing. When it comes to fighting the good fight, I am much more suited to signing an occasional petition . . . or clicking "like" on a Facebook page.

Besides, this is America, where everyone can make it with a little pluck and a little luck. Sure, growing up in a predominantly white suburb I had experienced insensitivity more than once (including some things I now know enough as an adult to be retroactively offended by), but I thought the world was changing—hell, even my little hometown was changing. The artistic director of the area's regional theater had adopted a colorblind casting policy. Certainly the New York TV, film, and theater worlds would be even more enlightened.

And when I got to New York I did the same bottom-tier paying-your-dues non-union gigs everyone does. I was an extra. I did bad student films. I was an extra in bad student films. I did one-act plays at midnight to an audience of seven. This was fun, creative, energetic, amazing . . . *actually* doing what I came to New York to do. But after a while, it became not fun. I was holding at semi-pro and wanted to get up to the majors. I needed to build up my credits. My game plan was to get my foot in the door with a reputable theater company in the hopes that legitimate television and film roles would follow.

At open casting calls, there would be a line around the block for the role of "Townsperson," but the competitive pool got significantly smaller for the role of "Cab Driver's Wife." I realized that the thing that was going to get my foot in the door was the thing I once thought would hold me back—being Indian. The illumination did not thrill me, especially since these characters were often one-dimensional or stereotypical, but I was more ambitious and had less perspective then. My attitude was: *I'll be whomever you think an Indian or South Asian American person is, just give me a job.* I watched a lot of *Simpsons* episodes to learn an Indian accent (which to this day is still bad), and landed a role in a workshop production of a play set in Mother Teresa's mission in Calcutta—produced by a small but notable theater company.

It was semi-autobiographical, written by a white playwright who, as a young man, wore himself out on the gay club scene. He left partying, drugs, and a multitude of casual lovers behind to volunteer in Calcutta. The protagonist arrives a broken man, seeking a sense of purpose by doing good. He meets other broken souls from other Western nations seeking the same. In the following order, he: finds friendship, receives sagacious wisdom from a dying beggar, is visited in a dream by the goddess Kali (me), is spiritually reborn, and is thus able to experience real love and intimacy by leading another self-hating gay volunteer out of the closet (with his words, not his penis).

Sounds convoluted and hokey, but it was beautiful. The dialogue was sheer poetry. The playwright was also a sensitive and gifted director. The workshop was well received. I hoped that even if the play didn't get a full production, I would be considered for other roles within the company.

I was, but not for the Lanford Wilson or the Craig Lucas play—for this same marginally known playwright. Which was marginally fine until I realized he was obsessed with India. Truly. Deeply. Hopelessly obsessed. He was so white he was borderline translucent, yet he saw himself as Indian by proxy. He was flummoxed when SALGA, the South Asian Lesbian and Gay Alliance, wouldn't let him join. Even Gauguin took a break from exoticizing Tahitian women to paint a horse or bowl of fruit every now and again.

But alas, I was working. The plays were lovely when considered alone and creepy only when you regarded the whole canon. During my tenure with that theater company I played a Bengali nun who provides spiritual wisdom and mystical illumination for the white character, the goddess Kali appearing in a dream to provide spiritual wisdom and mystical illumination for the white character, a Bengali lesbian who is murdered by her lover's husband, and a novice (nun-in-training) who provides spiritual wisdom and mystical illumination for the white character.

Through these plays I gained notice from actual South Asian and South Asian American playwrights and was cast in their plays' workshop productions as well. My roles shifted from Indian characters on the subcontinent to first-generation-born Americans with first-generation-born issues. The predominant themes were Culture Clashes with Parents; When East Meets West, Comedy Ensues; and Racism Hurts. Though racism does indeed hurt, I hated the Racism Hurts genre. First because I had no desire to be typecast as a victim, and second because it made me feel icky.

I'm of the generation of Indian Americans whose parents largely came here when the United States anticipated a professional labor shortage and not only permitted but solicited scientists, doctors, and engineers to immigrate. We grew up in colonials on tree-lined cul-de-sacs and were driven to soccer practice in minivans. Hardly the migrant workers César Chávez fought for. Hardly being tear-gassed and clubbed for the right to ride a bus, go to school, or be treated like a human being. Racism Hurts coming from us felt distasteful.

I grew weary of the theater scene. The pigeonhole I willingly crawled into was hardly better than not working. I was no longer engaged, challenged, or having any fun. I'd do a role . . . rinse . . . repeat. And no matter how hard I tried, I couldn't shake the sinking feeling that I was performing a long-lost cousin of the minstrel show. I cried to be led out of this dark pit of cliché and banality and was met by the hand not of art, but of commerce.

At that time, here's how things typically went: if a television or film breakdown (a casting call) went out for Wall Street types, agents and casting directors would send out clean-cut, blond, blue-eyed young men with chiseled features and size 40 regular suits, though anyone who's spent time at the corner of Wall and Broad Streets knows it's pretty diverse. If a TV or film breakdown went out for a wry waitress in my age range, though the character type is squarely in my wheelhouse, I would never get called in. Race would not have to be mentioned in the character description. White was understood to be the default. But if it was a commercial breakdown, the audition room would be more representative of the American population. Increasingly, commercial castings were either seeking all ethnic types or viewing race as unimportant. Not all advertisers, of course, but effective advertisers operate off of cold, hard demographic numbers and not preconceived notions or stereotypes. The only color they care about is green.

I managed to book a few things here and there. I don't know if that opened doors or if the industry was evolving, but auditions for non-stereotypical roles started to trickle in. I was second in line for a role on a sitcom pilot. I landed roles in two indie shorts, one as the best friend and one as a lawyer. I booked bit parts on a few soap operas. Baby steps, but baby steps in the right direction. Things seemed to be turning around.

Until September 11.

Nothing embodies the word "bittersweet" to me more than being a New Yorker on and after September 11—the "bitter" being the unfathomable losses suffered and the "sweet" being how the whole city came together in the face of it. I remember the graffiti that appeared on the sidewalk near my apartment: the towers encased in a heart with the words "we are all together." I remember walking down Grand Street when a sixty-year-old man in a yarmulke spotted a sixty-year-old Chinese man. From outward appearances, the two men would seem to be from different worlds, but they were friends who obviously had not seen each other since before the attack. They became emotional, embracing and saying how glad they were to see each other.

I also remember being the recipient of more smiles and small talk than is customary in New York City. Though people may have been saying, "Try the special, it's pretty good," or, "I like your hat," what they really were saying was *I see from your complexion you could be Middle Eastern. Whether you are or aren't is inconsequential to me, as I understand this atrocity was committed by a few terrorists, not an entire ethnic or religious group. I hope you have not experienced any resentment, my fellow New Yorker.* If I ever had a doubt, I now knew I lived in the greatest city in the world.

This is not what MTV wanted to hear.

In October 2001, about six weeks after the terrorist attacks, I was called by a producer at MTV to audition for a public-service announcement about racial tolerance in the wake of the tragedy. When I arrived in her office she asked me about the backlash I'd experienced.

"Yeah, I read some horrible stuff in the paper just this morning, but if anything, people have gone out of their way to be nice to me."

"Oh. Okay . . . then tell me about the ignorant comments you've heard."

"Uh, I haven't heard any."

"Are you sure you haven't been called a racial slur?" Apparently this woman, who was African American herself, had the great fortune of never having been called a racial slur. It's not something one easily forgets.

"Yes, I'm sure."

"Oh."

She was disappointed. I quickly realized the campaign was going to be made up of unscripted personal tales of racial intolerance. If I didn't come up with something, I wouldn't get the job. A PSA on MTV would be fantastic exposure and would look great on my reel. Besides, I needed the money. I had to think fast.

"Uh, when I lived in Connecticut strangers would often ask me where I was from. You know, as if I was a foreigner, despite the fact that I'd lived there since elementary school. I was born in the U.S. It was irritating."

She lit up. "Oh, good. Can I tape you talking about that?"

So, on camera, I talked about how I was a genuine Jersey-born U.S. citizen yet would be approached as if I were a foreigner. I told her about how in the high school marching band, inevitably someone from the opposing team's band would ask if I was a foreign exchange student (and I wasn't even doing the walk-like-an-Egyptian dance). I told her how two old ladies eating at the restaurant I waited tables at in college complimented me on my lovely tan. When I told them that I was Indian and therefore born dark-skinned, they marveled at how beautifully I spoke English and asked if I knew their priest, who was also Indian.

When doing a personal recounting, like with scripted work, you're playing a character. All characters need a narrative arc. My character was someone who's profoundly annoyed but then learns to find humor in uncomfortable situations. I did not play a victim. I left the office certain I would not book the job.

I booked the job and was called into the studio the next day. On set I met two other actors also taping a spot. The director, a curious cross between a *GQ* model and a used-car salesman, arrived and gave us a little vent-all-your-racism-stories pep talk. "So I want you to let it all hang out. Start on the mark but feel free to move around, because we have a close and a wide. Who wants to go first?"

The first to volunteer was Amit. Handsome, rugged—I imagined Amit was one of those guys who was torn between sports and drama in high school. He started by telling the story of how he received quite a bit of ribbing one time in high school. He'd shown up for baseball practice after a big family dinner. ". . . So then my friend Dan says, 'hey, man, you smell like curry.' And I did. The smell sticks to you, man. I was sweating it out my pores. Then . . . I started farting curry.

And the ventilation system in our locker room was not so good."

The director looked dismayed. "Can you just shorten the story and make it a question?"

"A question?"

"Yeah, just what your friend said about how you smelled. Just state it in the form of a question."

"You mean like *Jeopardy*?"

"Sure."

"What is—curry farts?"

"No, uh, how 'bout imitating your friend asking *why* do you smell like curry?"

"Oh, okay. 'Hey, man, why do you smell like curry?'"

"Great, great! Now do that a couple more times."

And so it went. The director teased a few more "questions" out of Amit, my favorite being "Do you know the *Kama Sutra*?"—asked of him by a girl in college as a barroom pickup, not as the racial putdown it was edited to seem like. As directed, Amit's spot ends on the scripted line "Are you a terrorist?" But Amit's devil-may-care personality still comes through despite the heaviness of the line.

Next up was Khalid. He had just moved to New York City from San Jose a few months earlier to pursue acting. For a newbie he caught on quick. He told the director, "You don't have to say anything. I've got my questions." Apparently, in addition to the best and the brightest, Silicon Valley is also home to the worst and the dimmest. Khalid had heard questions like "Do you live in a tent?" and "Do you have a camel?" A camel. In San Jose. California. Clearly Khalid was making this shit up. He came across as very sad in the finished product, especially on the last, "Are you a terrorist?" line. Khalid's PSA gets the most air play.

Then it was my turn. I tried to turn the anecdotes I told the producer into "questions," but the director quickly lost patience and started feeding me lines. The first one was "Where's your red dot?" Okay. Not so bad. I've actually heard that before. Then came "Does your husband beat you?" Which was doubly ridiculous, because at the time, I was a million years away from having a relationship that lasted even to breakfast the next morning (instead of riding the F train at the crack of dawn in sequins and smudged eyeliner). We ended with the ubiquitous "Are you a terrorist?" which of course was the goal of the whole campaign: to let people know that not all South Asian and Middle Eastern Americans were terrorists. Not a bad thing, right? On the racial tolerance issue I fall squarely in the "for" camp, but I felt . . . dirty. And couldn't put my finger on exactly why.

I wince when I see the PSA. It was snappily put together with music and quick cuts. It looks good. I look good, but I'm not "on voice," which in actor-speak means the pitch of my voice is unnaturally higher, whiny, and forced from the throat. I'm not grounded in my diaphragm and honestly connecting to the words. People mistakenly think acting is akin to lying, but it's really about being truthful—good acting is truthful behavior in made-up circumstances. In the PSA I come across as wounded and angry . . . a victim.

I wish I could say that the MTV incident was a standalone, but it wasn't. After 9/11 my acting career sort of languished. So I wrote. I wrote screenplays. I wrote teleplays. I wrote and produced a short film. I founded and curated a small comedy film festival. I kept myself busy, because The Business didn't seem to have a place for me. Besides my small recurring role on a soap opera, I didn't book much. Almost everything I auditioned for seemed to involve the theme of terrorism or be grossly stereotypical. I never managed to completely ditch that dirty feeling in order to do the ethnic shtick that was required of the roles. I'm sure many casting directors just assumed I was a bad actor.

After 9/11 there was fear. Fear of Muslims, fear of people who could be seen as "the other," and certainly fear of the unknown. At times like that, it's comforting to put people into nice, neat categories: the African American drug dealer, the Korean convenience store owner, the South Asian with terrorist ties.

For example, during World War II, when America needed women to contribute to the war effort and take over jobs men previously held, films featured an abundance of smart, fast-talking, spunky women like Rosalind Russell in *His Girl Friday*. When the men returned home, there was societal uncertainty over the roles of women in postwar America. That nervousness is reflected in the noir films of the time, in which the smart women were portrayed not as spunky and endearing, but as femme fatales—sexually dominant, emasculating, threatening, and often murderous. Art and society are opposite-hung mirrors that forever reflect each other. The phenomenon would have been fascinating if post-9/11 fears and anxiety were cock-blocking someone else's career.

Then the winds of history blew me again, but this time in a good way. In January 2008, Barack Obama won the Iowa Caucus. I think that this, even more than his eventually being elected president, changed public opinion. As *Time* magazine's Joe Klein said, "A black man with a dangerous-sounding foreign name trounced his opponents in the nearly all-white state of Iowa." If America could envision a black man as the leader of the free world, certainly they could see Americans of non-European heritage in any number of roles.

I'm certain I am not imagining that it seeped into the collective subconsciousness of the entertainment industry that they had been selling middle America short. Everyone along the chain of command within The Business had been selling everyone short, assuming prejudices that were not there: the agent doesn't submit the perfect African American actor for the Wall Street type because he doesn't think it will fly with the casting director. The casting director doesn't open it up because she doesn't think it will fly with the director or producer. The director or producer doesn't go out on a limb because they think it won't fly with the network. The network doesn't make changes they think won't fly in fly-over country. After Barack Obama won the Iowa Caucus, almost on cue, my career turned around.

No, I didn't become an international star, but I was getting auditions for roles that were more "me." And although stereotypical characters were far from extinct, I was able to ditch the chip on my shoulder and do better at those auditions, because I wasn't suffering from typecasting fatigue anymore. I was mostly being seen for characters where race was inconsequential, and most of the traditional Indian characters I got called in for were less one-dimensional.

Variety and dimensionality are really what made the difference. Unlike being a painter, a musician, or an architect, when you're an actor you can't totally escape your packaging. If you're fat or Indian or as tall as a pro basketball player, you're going to get called in for clichéd roles. But it's not so disheartening when those aren't the *only* roles you're being seen for. Moreover, fully fleshed out characters keep the conventional from becoming insulting. At first glance, the television series *The Wire* had all the worn-out crime drama clichés, complete with Irish cops and African American drug dealers, but it was anything but hackneyed because the characters were so multifaceted and portrayed with such depth and humanity.

Now many breakdowns include the footnote "We are committed to diverse, inclusive casting. For every role, please submit qualified performers, without regard to ethnic origin, unless otherwise specifically indicated." This is not to say that everything is all kumbaya and Shangri-la. The other day I saw a breakdown that said, "We are looking for this role to be diverse." This offended me more as an English major than as a person of color. Something can be diverse only in relation to something else. The word choice implied that white is the norm and anything else is a diversion from that.

It was probably written by a grammatically challenged assistant attempting to be politically correct, unaware that just coming out and saying "Not Caucasian" is not an insult to those of us who are not Caucasian.

Recently an independent producer became interested in a project of mine, a children's educational TV series I developed about a nine-year-old African American boy who unlocks the secret of a magic library and has adventures getting lost in the books. Beyond the initial pilot, I outlined future episodes, all involving events in U.S. and global history: the Rosetta Stone, World War II, Lewis and Clark, and so forth. An episode about the Harlem Renaissance was the only show out of the ten episodes involving what could be construed as a black theme. The show was hardly a children's cartoon version of *Roots*. But the producer wanted me to add a section to the series proposal to "be clear to point out that his adventures are not exclusively Afrocentric."

I may not have ditched that chip on my shoulder after all, because this made me feel icky. The fact that the show was centered around a broad range of historical themes was evident in the proposal. Was he asking me for the redundancy to *reassure* the network development executive? Was he fearful that the exec would be fearful that an African American protagonist would not be acceptable to fourth graders in middle America?

I decided not to give in to fear, to be of a post–Iowa Caucus mindset, and to give that development executive the benefit of the doubt. After all, at the time the head of that network was an African American woman. Dora the Explorer, a bilingual Hispanic character, was the hottest thing with the preschool set since Snoopy. I wanted to believe that the world had changed. And even if it hadn't, I wasn't going to change my proposal.

I've made the decision not to do anything that makes me feel icky, not out of any social justice-y high-minded principle, but simply because I don't want to. "Icky" is not enjoyable. "Icky" is not engaging. "Icky" is not challenging. And since I am not a big-name star or a brand with people relying on me for their income, I have the luxury of just pleasing myself. If I want money or fame there are easier ways to get it. Every job I do takes me away from my kid, puts strain on my family, and is an investment of my time, sweat, and tears. Those are not things to be squandered. When it comes to the incredibly sticky, uncomfortable, complicated, minefield-laden subject of race: "icky" is as good a gauge as any.

why my screenplay isn't finished

I AM LYING in bed . . . laying? Lying? I can never remember which is proper. I should look that up in my good ol' Strunk and White. It is now my official writing time. I should get out of bed. A designated writing time makes me a real screenwriter, as opposed to a dilettante. Though I have never sold anything, I am a real screenwriter with a real writing time. Which is now. But I am not writing now. I am still in bed. Mmmmm . . . I smell coffee.

That coffeemaker timer thing was the best money I have ever spent. I am also glad I buy the Gold Reserve Ethiopian Sumatran Blend for $37.50 a pound. I am a real writer and real writers deserve real coffee. Mmmmm. That is good. Back in the day, screenwriters put pen to tattered notebooks in greasy spoon diners . . . but there are no greasy spoons in Park Slope. And who can drink that percolated swill? Mmmmm. Gonna pour myself another cup of this good stuff—

Looks like a three-mug morning. Computer on and I am ready to go. Professional screenwriter. Me. Picking up on page three, where I left off yesterday—

        PERCY looks across the smoky pub, over
        the heads of the bawdy, boisterous ruffi-
        ans and sees her- PENELOPE, ~~30s~~. 20s. The
        most beautiful woman we've ever seen in
        the history of cinema-

I am writing myself a wonderful role in this screen-play. That will make me a star. That is what Matt and Ben did. That is what Stallone did. The studio loved *Rocky* so much they gave in to his demand to play the lead role, even though he was a total unknown (like me!). That is also what the lady from *My Big Fat Greek Wedding* did, and that was the highest-grossing movie that—

What was her name? Whatever happened to her? That's right; she did that film where she masqueraded as a drag queen because she was being chased by the mob and had to go into witness protection . . . or was that Whoopi Goldberg in *Sister Act?* No. Whoopi was a nun. The *Big Fat Wedding* girl was the drag queen. That movie tanked, but that won't happen to me. I will be like Matt and Ben.

What shall I wear to the Academy Awards? Valentino? Prada? Does Prada make gowns? I'm sure they must. What a silly thought. Or maybe I will wear something totally outrageous like Bjork's swan dress or the dress made from American Express Gold Cards. What shall I say in my speech? I have to thank the little people without making it seem as if I think of those people as little. Then I will seem humble and gracious and my fans will love me all the more!

WAIT! How did I get to President Street? I should be back at the apartment crafting my screenplay. I don't even remember putting my shoes on. Well, since I'm out here I might as well stop by my favorite café for an espresso shot and a pastry. I deserve it. I also deserve a laptop, but who can afford it with the price of coffee? I will buy a laptop after I sell my screenplay. This screenplay is going to turn my world into a big fat oyster.

I am not delusional. I know most screenwriters don't get any respect in the Hollywood studio system. Not like directors. I am a professional screenwriter and read about these things all the time in my professional screenwriter magazines. It's the opposite in television:

TV writers rule the roost. Except I am also an actor, and the pace of TV might not allow me to do both. Yeah, I'm a triple threat. I'm an actor, a writer, and . . . here I am. Maybe I will get two double macchiatos and two pastries. I haven't eaten anything all day. The life of an artist!

Ahhh. That really hit the spot. I will walk home and be revived for my writing. Look at all the poor schlubs going about their lives. The businesspeople. The hipsters. The mommies . . . When I get my Oscar I will carry it in a Baby Björn and walk all around Park Slope. I will pass the Park Slope mommies and smile with condescension—what do you have, a baby? A husband who keeps you in black-rimmed glasses? A Ph.D. in psycho-socio-post-modern philosophy from Berkeley? I may have flunked out of state school and have trouble making friends due to my social anxiety disorder, but I pity you. I pity your unfortunate-looking child. I pity your black-rimmed glasses. I pity your outfit that looks relaxed and accidentally hip yet costs as much as a Prius. I have an Oscar.

Okay. Back in my designated home office professional writing space, and it is time for me to get serious. Totally serious. Total cereal. I think I may be out of cereal. I am going to take a quick break and order my groceries.

Okay. That's done. Back to the drawing board.

```
The  obstreperous,  carousing  riff-raff
in the smoky pub is suddenly silenced,
overcome by her intense beauty. Penelope
and Percy lock eyes. She slowly saunters
toward him in her gorgeous Prada gown,
her heels click-clacking on the Spanish
terra cotta tile.
                   PENELOPE
                (seductively)
          Hello.
```

I don't know what to write next. That happens to all real writers. I'm sure even Woody Allen hits a roadblock sometimes. But what does a real writer do? I know I should do something. Maybe I should do one of those deep-breathing exercises, and the ideas will come to me. Hmmmm. Hmmmmm. Ohmmmmmm. Ohmmmmmm. Deep diaphragmatic breathing. Maybe I should go ahead and nap. Wake up refreshed. Then ideas will flow like the river Jordan . . .

This isn't working. I can't just lie (lie? lay?) here. I've had so much coffee it'll be a wonder if I sleep before Tuesday . . . Now what? Back to the computer! Because I am not a hack. No matter what anyone says. I am a goddamn professional screenwriter. Onward and upward! Back on that horse, young knave!

Boy, this computer is dirty. That is the problem with these white keyboards. I should clean it off. I mean, who would be able to write with a dirty keyboard?

There. That's better, but look at all that dust trapped inside. Where's that tiny screwdriver I bought to fix my black-rimmed glasses? I should just take this apart and get that dust out!

Now I can attack this screenplay. It is bad screenwriting feng shui to have a dirty workspace. I have got to finish this screenplay in time for that screenplay competition, which I will win and set this whole big ball into motion. I have so many other magnificent ideas. Maybe I should scrap this and work on my Kaufman-esque existential romantic comedy.

Five o'clock. Writing time is over. It is good to put in a full day. It is good to be an artist and not a working stiff punching a clock. Who are they to suggest I get a real job? I don't need no stinkin' real job. I spit on their real jobs. I am an artist, goddammit. e. e. cummings said it was the most awful responsibility on earth. Boy, ain't that the truth.

just say no . . .
or the curious case
of joan rivers

NEW AGE-ISH self-helpers warn against something called "scarcity mentality." Stephen Covey, author of *The Seven Habits of Highly Effective People*, explains the concept this way: "People with a scarcity mentality tend to see everything in terms of win-lose. There is only so much; and if someone else has it, that means there will be less for me." These New Age-ish self-helpers believe that it is this scarcity mentality framework of thinking, rather than an actuality of limited resources, that creates lack in one's life. Perhaps the theory bears out with intangibles like friendship, love, or recognition. But in regard to tangible assets like money, jobs, or natural resources, even the philosophy's most ardent subscribers would struggle to hold their position in a debate with an economist, a geophysicist, or an Actor, Writer, Whatever.

No calculator necessary. Actor, Writer, Whatevers far outnumber available gigs. Every audition waiting room is packed with women just like me—and only one of us is going to get the role. Work *is* scarce. The few occasions I have turned down work were dizzying, disorienting, and downright jarring—a voice in my head shrieking, *What the hell are you doing? You don't know when or if you'll work again! How can you turn down work?!*

For example, years ago I was asked to participate in a television magazine show for men. The name of the show escapes me . . . I think it was *Stud* or *Dude* or some other thinly veiled synonym for *Cock*. They wanted me to be a part of a segment where women shared their thoughts on men, dating, and sex. They weren't looking for a Camille Paglia versus Gloria Steinem class of discussion. It was to be a "young and fabulous single gals' night out" aesthetic. We would sit around a cocktail lounge set, drink cosmos, and talk about boys.

"How else will men know how women feel? What we want? How to please us?" the producer asked in a tone suggesting the show was a public service akin to bringing awareness to global warming or breast cancer. I'm sure my face betrayed this thought, because she quickly added, "And if you wind up saying something you regret, we can edit it out."

"Right," agreed the director, "just say to me, 'Kendra, that thing I said about the dildo, can you make it disappear?' and it's gone. Like it never happened."

A better way to make it "like it never happened" would be not to do the show in the first place, I thought.

I told them I would think about it. Not doing the show was a no-brainer, but I was not acclimated to this alternate universe of turning down work. *Could I possibly be missing some merit in doing the show?* I ran it over in my mind on the subway ride home. *Nope. Nothing redeeming about talking about dildos on television.* Any doors the show might open were not ones I wanted to walk through. When I got home I called and politely turned down the offer. Then I broke into a cold sweat and had to lie down with a moist cool washcloth over my face.

I've also turned down extra work . . . eventually. When I was brand-spanking new to New York those first phone calls booking paying jobs were incredibly exciting. I was an extra in films, commercials, and TV shows. Though on screen for a fraction of a nanosecond, I was thrilled to be on an episode of *Sex in the City*. But not as thrilled as my friend Nia. She taped it, and when my image streaked across the background she would freeze the frame, hoot, and clap her hands in sheer delight, then rewind and do the whole thing over again. I felt like a superstar.

The feeling didn't last long. I got sick of doing extra work, though I am still grateful for the experience. It taught me how sets work. When I finally got a job where I actually spoke, I was prepared. Through extra work I learned the lingo, how to hit my mark, and how to position myself in relation to the camera. I also learned that the "real" actors had the easiest, or the least physically demanding, jobs on set. The hours were shorter. They had dressing rooms. They were paid better. Extras do not enjoy these advantages. Extras are moving scenery . . . which makes them, in spirit, part of the art department. Worthy of respect, but in the art department nonetheless.

It's exhausting work for the longest hours and the smallest paycheck to be the lowest on the totem pole. If you seek a satisfaction beyond just being on camera and really want to *act* act, you have to stop doing it at some point. No one will take you seriously, and it's not good for your own morale. I felt like a Dickensian peasant pressing my nose against the bourgeois family's window at dinnertime.

The experience was past its expiration date, sour and curdling, but every time a casting director called

I just couldn't say no. Taking the next step was scary. Staying put, even on that bottom rung, felt safe. Until it didn't. On an independent film set, my credit card was stolen from my purse in the extras' holding area. I could have gotten jacked anywhere in New York City, but I took it as a sign. The next time a casting director called I simply said, "Thank you for thinking of me, but I'm not doing extra work anymore." Then I broke into a cold sweat and had to lie down with a moist cool washcloth over my face.

It didn't take as long to grow weary of being a vide-ho.* Close your eyes and imagine your mother shakin' her booty in some rapper's face—or drinking Alizé with said rapper in a hot tub in the Bronx. Go ahead. Close your eyes and picture it. You've gouged your eyes out but *still* see it, yes? This is something I can spare my child, thanks to my small breasts (at least by vide-ho standards). The directors always put me in the back. No one will ever be able to pick me out or recognize me.

Do not misunderstand me. I love hip-hop. I'm a feminist, but I can't stop dancing. And I was a good dancer, but not passionate enough to put in the effort to become *really* good. It just didn't seem worth it as, ironically, the hip-hop scene got seedier the more main-

---

* "Vide-" as in "video." "Ho" as in the affectionate diminutive for "whore."

stream it became. Luckily, just as I was preparing my moist cool washcloth I was accepted into the actors' union. Since most music videos are nonunion jobs, I became ineligible once I joined. And my short, happy life as a vide-ho came to a close.

After each of these instances, I worked again. The earth didn't open up and swallow my career whole. But that's a natural fear. Turning down work is hard because getting work is hard and careers do indeed get swallowed whole. All you can do is hope that, like Jonah in the whale, eventually you'll be spat out on shore—just ask Joan Rivers.

Plastic surgery—stands on the red carpet—throws her microphone in celebrities' faces rasping, "Who are you wearing?" Joan Rivers? you ask. Yep. *That* Joan Rivers. Many think of her as someone whose only talent lies in sustaining third-tier celebrity-dom. She had completely fallen off my radar until I was clicking around late one night during a bout of insomnia (plague of the wound-too-tight). I stumbled upon the documentary film *Joan Rivers: A Piece of Work*. Until then, I had forgotten how provocative and edgy and groundbreaking she once was. I forgot she played all the same Greenwich Village clubs as Woody Allen, Richard Pryor, George Carlin, and Lenny Bruce. I forgot Lenny Bruce was a huge fan of *hers*.

In my opinion, Joan Rivers is not seen as a comedy trailblazer in the same vein as Richard Pryor or Lenny Bruce because (a) she is not dead, (b) she never turns down work, (c) she wants to be taken seriously, and (d) you can't have it both ways.

She's not dead. Joan Rivers's material was revolutionary. She was a nice Jewish girl from Brooklyn talking about things nice Jewish girls from Brooklyn were not supposed to talk about. She got laughs instead of shocked silence, due to her exquisitely calibrated timing. It takes a tremendous amount of skill and talent and, dare I say, brilliance to do this. If instead of Lenny Bruce, it had been Joan Rivers found naked and dead at forty years old in her Hollywood Hills bathroom surrounded by a syringe and other paraphernalia, she would be a perfectly romantic figure, heralded as a comedic genius and a counterculture icon.

She would have joined the ranks of the other tortured soul genius icons, like Marilyn Monroe and Jim Morrison. People would be arguing over which was better, the Scorsese or the Coppola (Sofia) biopic about her. Her image would be on t-shirts, and books about her would line the shelves of independent bookstores. That's the nice thing about dying while you're young and hot and hip and cool. You go out on top of the world, adhering to the cardinal rule of showbiz: *always leave 'em wanting more.*

But alas, Ms. Rivers did not die and didn't want her career to stop at being a darling of the Borscht Belt or the Greenwich Village cabaret scene. She wanted mainstream success. She wanted to, in the parlance of Central Brooklyn, "blow up large, son" and worked ceaselessly until she graduated to bona fide celebrity-hood.

Once a star, she had a different job from performer or artist. Stars are products. Products need to be packaged, marketed, and sold. They need lawyers, agents, managers, assistants, and publicists. When Joan Rivers became a product she became a business, and with all the lovely spoils of being a successful business came all the responsibilities.

Every now and then, a TV show gets canceled because the star comes completely unhinged—abusing drugs, soliciting prostitutes, or just plain losing his shit. Joan Rivers does not allow herself such indulgences. Not only is she painfully aware that others depend on her for their livelihood, but she relishes treating them well, going so far as to send the children of her staff to private school (my résumé's in the mail).

At the point her career came crashing down, as all careers do if you stay in this business long enough (it's a scientific absolute, like the rising and setting of the sun), she was determined to keep working, keep others working, and keep living the lifestyle to which she'd become accustomed. She had to maintain the largeness to which she had blown up. She'd keep the lights on and the employees employed at all costs.

And the cost is, *she never turns down work*. Ever.

In the documentary, we see her on a conference call discussing commercial endorsements. She lets everyone know that she will not turn down work, that she will "do anything." She will knock her teeth out and sell denture cream. She will wear a diaper. This is not because she has a toothless pamper fetish—she wants the cash. Unfortunately, you can't be willing to wear a diaper and expect the reviewer from the *New York Times* not to be prejudiced by it and to pan your one-woman show. If Rivers was young and painfully handsome with a sexy, shaggy haircut, she might be called a Renaissance man. A quirky eccentric. Like the indie film actor who writes a children's book, puts out an album of country hits, or has a gallery showing of his watercolors. That's arty. Dentures and diapers are not.

And there's the rub.

She wants to be taken seriously, and you can't have it both ways. And she should be taken seriously. She should be respected. Her television and comedy tour credits are endless. She's written screenplays, plays, books, and for television. She was nominated for a Tony Award and has an Emmy Award and a few honorary doctorate degrees. With more than forty years in the business, she could sit on her laurels. She could perform by rote and still get laughs, but every week she's not traveling she's at a small comedy club testing new material and honing her act. She is a consummate professional who has put in her ten thousand hours of practicing her craft twenty times over.

In 1971 she cowrote and starred in the Broadway show *Fun City* which the critics smashed to powdery shards. In the film, she gets choked up talking about it. It wouldn't still be so painfully raw after forty years, despite all she's attained, if she weren't an Actor, Writer, Whatever in her heart. An artist. Sadly, *artist* and *celebrity* mix about as well as oil and water.

Life is simpler when you choose one path and stick to that path. Joan Rivers could have chosen to just be happy with wealth and fame. Sure, keep the comedy act sharp, but beyond that, who cares. Stand on the red carpet, cash the check, live the high life. But she wants to do theater. She wants to keep acting and to be respected for it.

And this is how Joan Rivers vacillates between

being my hero and being my cautionary tale. She still tries to have it all. With every bad review she could have quit. With every canceled show she could have quit. With every plastic surgery joke she could have quit (or she could have quit the plastic surgery—but I shouldn't judge), but performing is her calling. It's just what she does, and despite all the knockdowns she still puts herself out there in a way that leaves her vulnerable. This is so brave it stuns me.

But I'd still rather eat rice and beans for the rest of my life than do something cringeworthy just for money. I don't want a golden cage. But when, God willing, I'm at the point where I've been at this for as long as Joan Rivers has, who knows? I may change my mind. I may just want to keep working. Only time will tell. I do know I don't break out into a cold sweat when I turn down work anymore. I don't beat myself up about getting to the next level because, at this level of being a "nobody," I am free.

On my next bout of insomnia I again clicked around the channels and stumbled upon another big star, Michael J. Fox, being interviewed on the show *Inside the Actors Studio*. He is asked if there's a dream or goal he has yet to achieve . . . and his answer is the most exquisite gift.

Yeah, I don't know what it is yet but I know I do wake up curious . . . and there's a way I'll be able to communicate something or express something that I haven't discovered yet. I've been able to do it through acting in some ways I still don't understand. In terms of specific dreams, I'd like to write another book. I'd like to direct another film. I'd like to produce something on television that is different and says something new. I'd like to find some acting job that I really enjoy.

The great thing that I have in my life is that there is no imperative, which then puts the responsibility on me to do it at the right time, in the right way. But I'm not going to be forced into doing something I don't want to do. I don't know what it is but there's something—something cool to be done.

For all his fame and success, I already have the same career as Michael J. Fox. Yes, he doesn't have a day job and lives in a nicer apartment, but I share his ambitions and, right this very minute, have the ability and means to achieve all of them—just on a much smaller scale. But the joy of being deeply engaged in fulfilling work cannot be scaled down. The indescribable feeling of following a creative curiosity through to its conclusion cannot be scaled down. There's no imperative I do anything, either. I can always say no.

did i peak too soon?

THE PHRASE "Man, that album changed my life" has become increasingly rare in recent years. People don't listen to albums anymore, on any format. Now we stream music or click around from one MP3 to another. It's just as well: when I hear "Man, that album changed my life," I roll my eyes. I shouldn't, because rolling my eyes makes me a judgmental shit. It also makes me hypocritical, because I too have an album that changed my life.

When you're a teenager the music you listen to is more than just the music you listen to. It's an identity, a big part of the persona you packaged to sell to yourself and the world. Back then, I felt as if I had to *be* something, but what to choose? We lived just far enough from the city to limit clear radio reception and my options. Everything over our airwaves was either top-forty bubblegum hits (fun, but I didn't want to appear vacuous), classic rock from a few generations earlier (I liked the blend of melody and harmony, and the message of peace, love, and rebellion, but I hated the uniform—tie dye? Hooded pullovers made from hemp? Oh no), and what was called "alternative" music ("alternative" to . . . ? The other two stations, I'm guessing). This last was the closest match for me, with its driving beat and angst-y lyrics baring the soul. It was all very "I hate myself and I want you to know about it." Like most teenagers, I felt unique in my melancholy and self-loathing. It felt as if those bands were singing about me, and at first it felt good—like the musical equivalent of looking in the mirror. But I eventually grew bored with my reflection and turned my attention to other things.

Then in college I heard *3 Feet High and Rising*, the debut album of the hip-hop group De La Soul—a while after it was released, as it wasn't played on local stations (my college station only played the *alternative* to "alternative" music). When the word of mouth finally got around to me, one listen was all it took. I was hooked. I listened to it nonstop, played it for friends who played it for friends; we danced in dorm rooms and drove around town with no particular destination because we didn't want to turn the key and turn it off. Nothing angst-y here: it was a celebration and a revelation—not all substantive artists were melancholy, anguished, angry, or cimmerian. Some were smart and funny and liked to dance. That album was the first step from where I was to where I was going. *Man, that album changed my life.*

Apparently I wasn't the only one. In 2011 the Library of Congress inducted it into the National Recording Registry, stating the following:

> *Bucking hip-hop's increasing turn toward stark urban naturalism in the late 1980s, De La Soul released this upbeat and often humorous album to widespread acclaim in the U.S. and abroad. The trio—Kelvin Mercer (Posdnuos), David Jolicoeur (Trugoy) and Vincent Mason (DJ Maseo)—was ably assisted by producer Prince Paul (Paul Huston) who has reported that these were some of the most productive, creative and entertaining sessions he ever worked on. For the album, the group marshaled an astonishing range of samples that included not only soul and R&B classics by Otis Redding and the Bar-Kays, but also Steely Dan's "Aja" and cuts by Johnny Cash, Billy Joel, Kraftwerk, Hall and Oates, and Liberace. Perhaps the most far-flung sample is a snippet of New York Mayor*

Fiorello LaGuardia reading the comics over the radio in 1945.

De La Soul plays these almost one hundred samples like master virtuosos on a Stradivarius, jazz greats scatting, or seasoned circus performers with ten plates spinning in the air. In the language of critics, the album was "experimental," but it feels less like an experiment and more like play . . . little boys unsupervised in the backyard. And what emerges from that random romping is a bike ramp, a rocket, or perhaps a trip to the emergency room (well worth it, of course, because it was all great fun).

It feels like play because the musicians were children. Well, not children exactly, but teenagers: three kids having a good time in the studio. The result is idealistic, fun, wild, youthful—definitely youthful. It embodies that phase in our lives when everything is new and untried: "Let's try this!" and "Why not?"

But when you get to a certain age, you know why not. You think about critics and audience and context. You think about the rules. You think about the bills. You worry about getting sued before you sample that album (*3 Feet High and Rising* changed the legal ramifications of sampling as well). There's a freedom to youth. There's play. That sense of play doesn't get lost as Actor, Writer, Whatevers mature, but it does get tempered.

There's a scientific basis for this change. As the neurobiologist Robert Sapolsky discusses in his essay "Open Season," younger people are simply more "amenable to novelty." Sapolsky goes on to say that studies measuring the output of creative types as varied as composers, poets, and research scientists have shown that "you'll find a decline after a certain, relatively youthful peak."

Damn. But wait . . . what exactly is "youthful"? Teens? Twenties? Did I miss my peak? Am I about to peak now? Is the peaking point different for everyone? I don't remember peaking. Could I have possibly peaked and missed it? That can't be the sort of thing that goes unnoticed, can it? Am I never going to be as good as the peak that I had but don't remember having? A peak should, by its very nature, stand out, right? And if I was peaking at some point in the past, and didn't capitalize on it, or get industry notice while peaking, is that it for my career? If a person peaks in the forest and no one discovers them, does it make a sound?

I feel dizzy.

Before I head to the store to stock up on pretzels and peppermint schnapps for the pity party honoring my rare achievement of attaining "has-been-dom" before "is-ness," another question occurs to me: Are all those poems and songs produced during that "youthful peak" any good? Given the "10,000 hours of practice to gain mastery" rule, shouldn't work get better with age and experience?

The most scientific study I'd conducted to date was testing the "beer before liquor, never sicker; liquor before beer, in the clear" theory—and that was back in (state) college. Incidentally, my findings showed that puke often resulted regardless of the order of consumption (the factor that appears to weigh more heavily is the volume consumed, though please keep in mind this was not a longitudinal study, nor were the results replicated in subsequent studies with any consistency). But I've read *Freakonomics* and a whole buncha Malcolm Gladwell books. I decide to throw down with those mofos* and do a study of my own.

I take the American Film Institute's choices for the hundred greatest films of all time and look to the Internet Movie Database to calculate the age of the director (within eleven months) at the time of each film's release:

---

* Mofo *noun* \moh-foh\ Diminutive for "motherfucker." Though sometimes used as a pejorative, it is oft used as a term of adoration and respect: *Chip only started playing golf a year ago, and that mofo got a hole in one!*

	Movie	Director	Year Film Released	Age
1	Citizen Kane	Orson Welles	1941	26
2	The Godfather	Francis Ford Coppola	1972	33
3	Casablanca	Michael Curtiz	1942	56
4	Raging Bull	Martin Scorsese	1980	38
5	Singin' in the Rain	Stanley Donen Gene Kelly	1952	28 40
6	Gone with the Wind	Victor Fleming	1939	50
7	Lawrence of Arabia	David Lean	1962	54
8	Schindler's List	Steven Spielberg	1993	47
9	Vertigo	Alfred Hitchcock	1958	59
10	The Wizard of Oz	Victor Fleming	1939	50
11	City Lights	Charles Chaplin	1931	42
12	The Searchers	John Ford	1956	62
13	Star Wars	George Lucas	1977	33
14	Psycho	Alfred Hitchcock	1960	61
15	2001: A Space Odyssey	Stanley Kubrick	1968	40
16	Sunset Boulevard	Billy Wilder	1950	44
17	The Graduate	Mike Nichols	1967	36
18	The General	Clyde Bruckman Buster Keaton	1926	32 31
19	On the Waterfront	Elia Kazan	1954	45
20	It's a Wonderful Life	Frank Capra	1946	49
21	Chinatown	Roman Polanski	1974	41
22	Some Like It Hot	Billy Wilder	1959	53
23	The Grapes of Wrath	John Ford	1940	46
24	E.T.: The Extra-Terrestrial	Steven Spielberg	1982	36
25	To Kill a Mockingbird	Robert Mulligan	1962	37
26	Mr. Smith Goes to Washington	Frank Capra	1939	42
27	High Noon	Fred Zinnemann	1952	45

	Movie	Director	Year Film Released	Age
28	All About Eve	Joseph L. Mankiewicz	1950	41
29	Double Indemnity	Billy Wilder	1944	38
30	Apocalypse Now	Francis Ford Coppola	1979	40
31	The Maltese Falcon	John Huston	1941	35
32	The Godfather Part II	Francis Ford Coppola	1974	35
33	One Flew over the Cuckoo's Nest	Milos Forman	1975	43
34	Snow White and the Seven Dwarfs	David Hand (Supervising Director)	1937	37
35	Annie Hall	Woody Allen	1977	42
36	The Bridge on the River Kwai	David Lean	1957	49
37	The Best Years of Our Lives	William Wyler	1946	44
38	The Treasure of the Sierra Madre	John Huston	1948	42
39	Dr. Strangelove	Stanley Kubrick	1964	36
40	The Sound of Music	Robert Wise	1965	51
41	King Kong	Merian C. Cooper Ernest B. Schoedsack	1933	40 40
42	Bonnie and Clyde	Arthur Penn	1967	45
43	Midnight Cowboy	John Schlesinger	1969	43
44	The Philadelphia Story	George Cukor	1940	41
45	Shane	George Stevens	1953	49
46	It Happened One Night	Frank Capra	1934	37
47	A Streetcar Named Desire	Elia Kazan	1951	42
48	Rear Window	Alfred Hitchcock	1954	55
49	Intolerance	D.W. Griffith	1916	41

	Movie	Director	Year Film Released	Age
50	The Lord of the Rings: The Fellowship of the Ring	Peter Jackson	2001	40
51	West Side Story	Jerome Robbins Robert Wise	1961	43 47
52	Taxi Driver	Martin Scorsese	1976	34
53	The Deer Hunter	Michael Cimino	1978	39
54	M*A*S*H	Robert Altman	1970	45
55	North by Northwest	Alfred Hitchcock	1959	60
56	Jaws	Steven Spielberg	1975	29
57	Rocky	John G. Avildsen	1976	41
58	The Gold Rush	Charles Chaplin	1925	36
59	Nashville	Robert Altman	1975	50
60	Duck Soup	Leo McCarey	1933	37
61	Sullivan's Travels	Preston Sturges	1941	43
62	American Graffiti	George Lucas	1973	29
63	Cabaret	Bob Fosse	1972	45
64	Network	Sidney Lumet	1976	52
65	The African Queen	John Huston	1951	45
66	Raiders of the Lost Ark	Steven Spielberg	1981	35
67	Who's Afraid of Virginia Woolf?	Mike Nichols	1966	35
68	Unforgiven	Clint Eastwood	1992	62
69	Tootsie	Sydney Pollack	1982	48
70	A Clockwork Orange	Stanley Kubrick	1971	43
71	Saving Private Ryan	Steven Spielberg	1998	52
72	The Shawshank Redemption	Frank Darabont	1994	35
73	Butch Cassidy and the Sundance Kid	George Roy Hill	1969	48
74	The Silence of the Lambs	Jonathan Demme	1991	47

	Movie	Director	Year Film Released	Age
75	In the Heat of the Night	Norman Jewison	1967	41
76	Forrest Gump	Robert Zemeckis	1994	43
77	All the President's Men	Alan J. Pakula	1976	48
78	Modern Times	Charles Chaplin	1936	47
79	The Wild Bunch	Sam Peckinpah	1969	44
80	The Apartment	Billy Wilder	1960	54
81	Spartacus	Stanley Kubrick	1960	32
82	Sunrise	F. W. Murnau	1927	39
83	Titanic	James Cameron	1997	43
84	Easy Rider	Dennis Hopper	1969	33
85	A Night at the Opera	Sam Wood	1935	52
86	Platoon	Oliver Stone	1986	40
87	12 Angry Men	Sidney Lumet	1957	33
88	Bringing Up Baby	Howard Hawks	1938	42
89	The Sixth Sense	M. Night Shyamalan	1999	29.
90	Swing Time	George Stevens	1936	32
91	Sophie's Choice	Alan J. Pakula	1982	54
92	Goodfellas	Martin Scorsese	1990	48
93	The French Connection	William Friedkin	1971	36
94	Pulp Fiction	Quentin Tarantino	1994	31
95	The Last Picture Show	Peter Bogdanovich	1971	32
96	Do the Right Thing	Spike Lee	1989	32
97	Blade Runner	Ridley Scott	1982	45
98	Yankee Doodle Dandy	Michael Curtiz	1942	56
99	Toy Story	John Lasseter	1995	38
100	Ben-Hur	William Wyler	1959	57

The average age of all directors:	42.88
The average age of directors of films in the AFI's top ten:	45.7

When I break down the directors' ages by decade, I come up with this:

Films with directors in their sixties:	4
Films with directors in their fifties:	16
Films with directors in their forties:	48
Films with directors in their thirties:	31
Films with directors in their twenties:	5

From these statistics I should feel encouraged. Maybe my best work is yet to come . . . then I notice something that sinks my mood again:

Films with directors of color:	2
Films with directors with vaginas:	0

Shit. Turns out, instead of feeling old while I was still young, I should have been focusing my neurosis elsewhere. But I am not good at multitasking. I am already obsessing over the age thing, so I put obsessing over the gender and color thing in my calendar for later in the week. I turn my focus back to the directors who have four or more films on the list (directors whose films would be the product of a consistently high work quality, rather than one-hit wonders) to see if their films got better or worse rankings with age.

Steven Spielberg

AFI Ranking	Film	Age
8	Schindler's List	47
24	E.T.: The Extra-Terrestrial	36
56	Jaws	29
66	Raiders of the Lost Ark	35
71	Saving Private Ryan	52

Alfred Hitchcock

AFI Ranking	Film	Age
9	Vertigo	59
14	Psycho	61
48	Rear Window	55
55	North by Northwest	60

Stanley Kubrick

AFI Ranking	Film	Age
15	2001: A Space Odyssey	40
39	Dr. Strangelove	36
70	A Clockwork Orange	43
81	Spartacus	32

Billy Wilder

AFI Ranking	Film	Age
16	Sunset Boulevard	44
22	Some Like It Hot	53
29	Double Indemnity	38
80	The Apartment	54

I only got a C in Statistics, but the one discernable pattern I could find was that not one of these heavy hitters did his best work at his youngest. Alfred Hitchcock did all his best work after the age of fifty-five. Alfred was a senior peaker. Encouraging news for those of us who get older every day *(hooray!)*. However, the AFI's pick for the number-one slot was directed by the youngest director *(boo!)*. Orson Welles wrote and directed *Citizen Kane* at twenty-six years old. But at the end of his life and career he was peddling screw-top wine in corny commercials. Perhaps there's something to not peaking too soon.

That is not to say that a great work created by a young person is always a fluke or of lesser merit. For example, Jonathan Safran Foer, Zadie Smith, and Michael Chabon all had successful novels in their twenties and continue to produce acclaimed or bestselling work. But Harper Lee published *To Kill a Mockingbird* in her early thirties, considered young for a Pulitzer

Prize–winning novelist, and hasn't published a word since. Maybe *To Kill a Mockingbird* and other wildly successful works by fledgling artists are akin to the Big Bang: a perfect alchemy of youthful energy, lack of self-consciousness, and experimentation that produces something completely surprising and astonishing. The tenderfoot artist is then left with the expectation to create another work of that velocity without fully understanding how she created the first work.

The Big Bang artist also hasn't had enough time to develop a technique or methodology to approach the act of *working*, every day, inspired or not. A more practiced Actor, Writer, Whatever has suffered through thousands of scrapped drafts, performances that fell short, and projects that went nowhere, but we still work consistently because it's an ingrained habit. We are accustomed to working without notice and don't expect lightning-in-a-bottle results. Years of practice may not have produced a Big Bang for me, but I know how to work, and when I stumble upon something good I know how to disregard any paralyzing thoughts like *I'll never be able to do this again.*

More than a few independent films have used a novice or non-actor who delivers a raw and compelling performance. The critics rave, the industry buzzes, and he wakes up as the Next Big Thing. Then he doesn't seem quite the same in the second film, and by the third film, tension and self-consciousness radiate off the screen . . . and the Next Big Thing disappears as quickly as he appeared, not having the know-how to sustain the spark.

I feel good about all of these discoveries. Then I feel bad. I feel as if I'm the only person on the planet any of this has occurred to. Nobody wants a young or inexperienced surgeon to do their emergency open-heart surgery. But Actor, Writer, Whatevers and just about everything else—yes. Even though you're better, no one will know it because they are paying attention to the younger, hipper, and/or more beautiful Actor, Writer, Whatever.

Youth is where it's at. And don't bother getting started on all these great recent television roles for women over thirty-five, because those women were already famous. You get a pass for going through the normal aging process if you were once a well-known hottie. You would think that writers would also get a pass, because nobody sees them, but they don't. They just don't. I assumed a country founded by Puritans would value, even in their artists, the principles of hard work, perseverance, and long, sustained dedication to one's vocation. But alas, it seems the other part of the American psyche is held in higher esteem: the plucky gold-rusher with a fire in his belly, hankering to get rich quick.

Almost a decade ago I produced, wrote, directed, and starred in an Off-Off-Off-Off-Off Broadway play. It enjoyed a sold-out run that sold out just by word of mouth, but not one critic saw it and it begat no future opportunities. I go back and read it and see that it's good: funny dialogue, compelling characters . . . but not as smart or well constructed as my current work. It feels less weighty . . . slightly frivolous. But it does have a certain something that my current work doesn't. It's wild. Energetic. Fun. I don't think it's a quality I could sustain. If it had been heralded as a Big Bang I suspect that I, like Orson Welles, would end my career hawking someone's wares in cheesy commercials. Even De La Soul, who continue to be a critics' favorite, have never reached the success of *3 Feet High and Rising*, per-haps because their later work doesn't elicit the same vis-ceral response.

And this is why I'm equal parts intrigued and irri-tated when I hear about the latest Actor, Writer, What-ever hovering around twenty-five, the hottest thing off the festival scene and christened brilliant. Most of these are extremely bright and talented. I hear them in inter-views saying bright and talented things, but without having lost that adolescent tendency to end their sentences a pitch higher. Everything sounds like an interrogative. It's as if they're seeking confirmation of what they already know—*they're the shit*. And they are. We all are when we're young. And that's the De La Soul of it.

what could
possibly happen?

I LIVE IN a small space. My husband, daughter, and I share a 715-square-foot apartment in Brooklyn: roughly one-third the size of the average American home. There are many perks to this. Less to clean, out-of-town guests don't overstay their welcome, and we're drawn out of our own doors to share the city with fellow New Yorkers of all stripes. Some would see this as a drawback, but it is one of the things that keeps me madly in love with this city. Instead of crocheting in front of my television, I meet a knitting group at a wine bar. Instead of a fenced-in backyard, we roam 585 acres of parkland designed by Frederick Law Olmstead and Calvert

Vaux. Instead of working in a home office, I work at the library or at a café.

I love the library. Unlike in cafés, I don't have to spend money or gain calories to be there. (I always submit to the most sinful sugar-and-carb-laden temptation. I so admire Eve for holding out as long as she did. I'd be off-and-a-chompin' on that apple before the serpent opened his mouth.) Also, the library is quiet. Mostly. Sometimes a patron will pick up his cell phone and proceed to have an endless conversation at a very un-library-like volume. Once in a while the music in someone's earphones will be playing so loudly that everyone else can hear the high tones (the resulting noise is most vexatious; thin and tinny, like a mosquito crooning on a transistor radio).

But these are the exceptions. Most, especially the regulars, are considerate. There's the guy who appears to be a graphic designer of some kind; he chews on toothpicks all day. There's the girl who is clearly in med school, with anatomy books piled high and flipping through flashcards. There's the guy with Tourette's who sits way off in the corner so as to not disturb anyone. (I didn't throw that last one in for comedic effect—you know, so you'd imagine a guy sitting in a pin-drop-silent library, intermittently shouting,

"COCK PECKER PRICK PISS PUSSY!!!!!" For your information, the exclaiming-obscenities tic occurs in a very small number of people with Tourette's. The majority just have a facial tic, like blinking, clearing their throat, or coughing. This may or may not be accompanied by emitting a small noise. Many successfully control their tics with medication. You may know someone afflicted and not realize it. It is a very misunderstood disorder.)

Did I sound defensive? Sorry. It's odd, but I feel a sense of camaraderie with the regulars. It's like working in an office with people you see every day yet your only communication is a silent gesture asking to watch your stuff while you go to the bathroom. And, truth be told, I have no idea if this guy's condition is Tourette's, or if he has any condition at all for that matter. I've been diagnosing him myself. He just sniffs and coughs a lot. A severe allergy sufferer perhaps? Whatever it is, I wish him well.

I have no such sense of comradeship at cafés. I work there only when the library is closed or if I want to read a script out loud (my voice blends in with a café's ambient hum and won't disturb anyone). People-watching can distract me, so in the mornings I choose a place off the beaten path to the subway.

One morning it's just me and another silent laptoper sitting at tables in the café, but the place still feels busy. The customers in line for coffee are engaging the counterperson in far more chitchat than is customary in pre-caffeinated New Yorkers. I look up to realize why: 97 percent of the line is male and the girl behind the counter is adorable. Absolutely adorable.

She's a kooky little twentysomething. Pretty, but not glamorous. The hipster version of the girl next door. Perfect for that dash of flirtation with your morning coffee—though it's only the customers who are doing the flirting. She's being herself, which just happens to be crazy charismatic and charming, thus making her all the more fetching.

I look at her and think, *I used to be you. I was quirky and comely. I was the girl at the coffee counter, behind the bar, the temp at the office. I was you before I learned too much to blithely skip through my days.* No one but the truly creepy flirts with me now. I'd like to blame the wedding ring or my un-Botoxed forehead, but I can't. I'm not in my twenties, but I'm still marginally attractive. It's the cynicism. Though not as repellent as its stepbrother, Bitterness, people smell it on you. Cynicism is not sexy. Hell, Realism is not sexy. Hope. Optimism. Expectancy. Sexy. Sexy. Sexy.

I would hate this girl if I, too, didn't find her to be so damn cute.

The morning marches on. The crowd thins. There's only one admirer, an obvious regular, at the counter, and she says to him, "Guess what? I just got a development deal."

"A what?"

"A development deal to make a TV show."

"Cool . . . Are you still going to work here?"

"Of course, silly. I need the material. Well . . . I'll be here until it gets picked up."

Okay, so now I hate her.

And then I feel bad about it—for not wishing this stranger well, even if in my own head. It will be an appropriate comeuppance to one day click on the television and say, *There she is. Six months ago she was pulling my espresso shot. Now she's a star and I'm unemployed. Ah, the whirligig of time.*

I don't feel inadequate and envious for long. Thankfully, the only successful people I resentfully ruminate over are douchebags, and this woman is unbearably sincere and very sweet. Other than that, she's probably not that different from myself. After all, we both came to New York with a purpose and a pursuit, and, as E. B. White said, "No one should come to New York to live unless he is willing to be lucky."

We are all willing, but she was lucky.

Very lucky.

It is seemingly impossible to get an opportunity to be one of the thousands to pitch a show idea to the networks each year. I gather from my deductive powers of eavesdropping that she bypassed this painful step, as someone-who-is-someone approached her after reading her blog. Hers will be one of the hundreds of projects that will go into development this year. Of those, about one in twelve will get made into a pilot, and an even smaller percentage will get picked up. Math doesn't lie. The odds are the show will go nowhere.

Now I feel sad. I don't want her to fail. I just don't want to know about her success.

But who knows? Maybe her dreams won't get dashed. Maybe the end-of-innocence-you-can-never-go-home-again-perhaps-I'm-just-not-*destined*-for-greatness-and/or-stardom-and-that-blows-like-a-broke-crack-whore moment is not in her future. Maybe the network will like her treatment. Maybe it will even catch the eye of the network president. Maybe the network president will present it to a Big Movie Star who just happens to be looking for a television project.

But maybe she won't be sure if this particular Big Movie Star is exactly the right fit, because maybe her show is about her and her purposely unpolished friends working in a café while trying to break into various artsy-fartsy professions—and the Big Movie Star is, well, a big movie star. But maybe, even though she's a total neophyte, she's savvy enough to know that if the Big Movie Star wants to do the show it will definitely get green-lit!

And maybe it happens. Big Movie Star does like it. Maybe the executive actually said Big Movie Star "loved," not "liked," it but she downgrades it in her head because love means never having to change and they want to change a few things. She doesn't yet know what all these things are going to be, but she is guaranteed that they are just "little tweaks." One of the little tweaks is that she has to move to Los Angeles.

Maybe this is fine, exciting, wonderful. What's not to like about L.A.: great weather, beach volleyball, burritos. But maybe hers is a New York story and Brooklyn is essentially one of the characters. Maybe she asks herself, *Will it work in L.A.? Or will it feel canned, prepackaged, potboiler?* Maybe it's most important to her that it maintains its rough, gravelly quality——so it feels like watching a funny half-hour independent film. Maybe she expresses this to the executive, who assures her, "Don't worry! Think of *Friends*. It was shot in L.A. and was the biggest hit ever!" She gets the feeling he didn't quite hear her and missed the point completely. Maybe it briefly occurs to her that she gets that feeling a lot lately.

Maybe in L.A., it's meeting after meeting—including meeting Big Movie Star and the network chief for lunch at a restaurant she could never afford to even walk past in her previous café-counter-girl manifestation. Big Movie Star is just as handsome in person. Maybe she never thought of herself as someone who would be impressed by such things, but her heart beats fast. Her pits dampen and her palms sweat. Maybe she keeps her cool but is relieved when he leaves early for another meeting.

Maybe she and the network chief continue the lunch, which mostly consists of him raving about the show. When they are about to leave, he asks, "Does it have to be a coffee shop?"

She's a bit thrown, but answers, "Well . . . my blog is about people in a café. You know, the people who work there, the customers, the relationships they form. It's safe, warm, comforting, you know, like coffee. The whole show is sort of a metaphor for a coffee break—a respite from the harsh reality of pursuing dreams in the big city, but rejuvenating and energizing too."

"Well, yes! Of course! Let's keep all that, because it's fabulous! Really. Fabulous. But just not the coffee part. You don't want people to compare it to *Cheers*."

"I thought *Cheers* was a bar."

"Oh. Right. Well, you'll work on it . . . How about pizza? Everyone loves pizza."

"Well I—" She would finish her thought, but his cell phone rings.

She sits awkwardly while he has a conversation equal to the running time of all four operas in Wagner's Ring Cycle (if you played *Götterdämmerung* twice.)

Finally he hangs up and turns back to her. "You were saying something?"

"Oh, uh . . . I forget. Probably not important."

They say their goodbyes, but not before he tells her just shy of twenty more times how much he loves the script and how she's going to be "a big star star star!"

And maybe she really did forget what she was going to say, but she has a gnawing feeling it was, in fact, important.

So maybe she tries to remember this important thing as she drives back to her beautifully appointed bungalow in her beautifully appointed SUV, which she drives at forty-five miles an hour on the freeway. She hasn't driven since she traded in her car in Council Bluffs, Iowa, for the New York City subway. The traffic makes her nervous. It briefly occurs to her that everything makes her nervous since coming to L.A., but then—HOOOOONNNKKKKKK!!!! A passing driver flips her the finger—and the thought is gone.

Maybe she makes the change. It's now a pizza place. She makes a few other changes the network wants too. *What's the difference? I don't need to be rigid over the little things, because the core is still there: Brooklyn up-and-comers trying to "make it."* And maybe this makes her smile. *Hey, <u>I've</u> made it, right? Something I've written, a show about my life, is going to be on television . . . well, not quite my life, because I never worked at a pizza joint and I lived in Brooklyn not Queens and while I'm thinking of it I may not be all that crazy about the actors they're bringing in—too good-looking. My thing is about a ragtag sort of bunch.* Maybe it briefly occurs to her she should speak up about this, but in the end the beautiful and even more beautiful are cast.

Maybe she doesn't feel the pain of these thousand cuts and compromises until the pilot screening party. The first jab comes with the opening titles, when she sees the showrunner's name is alongside hers under the "created by" credit. This guy "created" jack shit, but the network told her over and over again how she was lucky he was even interested in her show while, in typical Hollywood euphemistic parlance, pointing out her lack of experience. Delicately implying that her running the show herself would be akin to a chimpanzee flying an airplane full of nuns and babies. It briefly occurs to her that she may have been manipulated into fearing the show would crash and burn without him, and thus sharing the "created by" credit (his contract stipulation). But then maybe the other thing that bothers her about the pilot hits her—

Which is that it's bad.

As in, not funny. Not smart. Not good. Bad. But maybe everyone at the pilot screening keeps congratulating her and telling her how "funny" and "groundbreaking" it is. She can't gauge anything for herself anymore.

So maybe she takes the tape home to watch it without the network's voices in her head. *Yep. Definitely bad . . . How did this happen?* Maybe only then does she realize that God is in the details. All the little changes add up to her nightmare of a hackneyed show. But maybe instead of being defeated by this, the spirit of the spunky girl who had men lined up out the café door returns. Full of vim and vigor, pluck and moxie, she decides to take control. Get this ship back on course. *Sure, this isn't my vision, but I can still find something to make my script's evil spawn into a show that's interesting and worth watching. A show I'd be proud of.*

Maybe since they told her she was brilliant six hundred times a day, she assumed her opinions would be accepted and respected. She isn't prepared for the blowback when she stops being the girl who goes along to get along. First they seem to listen, then it becomes a gentle "Honey, these people know what they're doing." But when she's unyielding, it escalates to knock-down drag-out fights—with the showrunner, the network, the producers, everyone. She cries on the drive to the studio, has a good sob on set in the middle of the day, and then again all the way home.

Maybe she goes to Big Movie Star seeking an ally, since they have an equal stake in the quality of the show. Maybe in her fragile state her guard and good senses are down and they wind up sleeping together. The next day Big Movie Star doesn't even pay her the courtesy of feigning awkwardness; the encounter was no more consequential to him than a cup of coffee. He doesn't speak to the network or producers on her behalf. It's business as usual—

Until she gets fired.

Maybe she feels humiliation and relief in equal measure as the security guard escorts her off the set. Maybe her lawyer assures her that she's guaranteed residuals for life, as she still shares the "created by" credit, but the riches don't roll in because the show is canceled after two episodes. This is disappointing but not a surprise since the show was, as one critic said, "the TV equivalent of a colonoscopy without the benefit of disease prevention."

Maybe even after this whole debacle she stays in L.A. and tries to make something happen. It doesn't. Maybe she starts drinking. Falls in with company she would never before keep. Her friends in New York were scrappy go-getters. These people are bitter, but then again, now so is she. They cloak their sourness in knockoff dresses and black eyeliner and head to the clubs. Maybe on one such night, she meets an actor she recognizes whose career has also hit the skids. Kindred spirits. They go home together. They stay holed up in his apartment for a week, surviving only on sex, cheap takeout, and conversation. The pillow talk peaks with the decision to move to Boulder, Colorado, to study massage therapy (him) and brewing beer (her). And maybe they do, but not before stopping in Vegas to get married.

Maybe marital bliss doesn't last long. The roller coaster runs from hot to cold, fire to ice, until eventually the fighting eclipses everything. She is every minute on the verge of tears until one day his agent calls. A Famous Director saw him in something he did years ago and offers him the lead in his next film. He returns to L.A. to claim his comeback. Since they had no marital assets, the divorce is handled by one of those Internet lawyers for two hundred and ninety-nine dollars. They split the cost.

Maybe she rebounds with a guy she meets while working at a microbrewery on Pearl Street. Maybe she follows this one to Humboldt, California. They open an Etsy shop selling a peppermint and sweet wood-ruff artisanal organic herbal tea that they grow, blend, and attractively package. Maybe it's simply delicious, but they still need to supplement their income by selling artisanal organic marijuana. Maybe, though happy for a spell, their relationship also turns tumultuous but does not play out to its moribund conclusion because they get arrested.

She pleas to a sentence of three years.

And maybe, yes, she suffers all the indignities incarceration has to offer. Prison is as filthy, degrading, and dehumanizing as she imagined. But what she did not imagine is making dear friends (who, ironically, are not bitter like her L.A. friends) and gaining clarity and comfort from the sparseness and the routine of prison life. Maybe she adopts a disciplined practice of exercising and writing before beginning her work in the prison kitchen, and then edits and rewrites until bedtime. Maybe she finishes her memoir just as she is released.

Maybe she gets a job at a food processing plant through a "Jail to Jobs" program. After each day of backbreaking work, she returns to the halfway house to stay up all night crafting query letters to literary agents. Unlike with the blog, this time around she is not "discovered" or "lucky." Instead she receives a shocking number of rejection letters before one agent finally calls.

Maybe once the memoir is published, both critics and readers embrace it. It becomes a bestseller. Maybe a producer approaches her to develop the show for a cable network. She's apprehensive for obvious reasons. The producer insists he is more than happy for her to maintain creative control. She doesn't believe him and so writes all the scripts for the first season. Take them or leave them. As is.

He takes them enthusiastically. In fact, later, he says in an interview, "I think that's why the show has been successful. Her voice is the through-line. She puts her stamp on everything: wardrobe, casting, sets. Everything."

Maybe she wins an Emmy—walks past her ex-husband to accept the award and thinks, *Whirligig of time, indeed.*

Then maybe she meets—

"Another?"

"Uh, what?"

She's standing at my table, clearing my empty cup. Like a hologram. My fantasy of this woman is more real than the human being standing in front of me. I am shocked she is not ten years older.

"Another coffee?"

"Oh, no thanks. I was just leaving." I pack up my stuff and head for the library. I have just two hours of writing time left before I have to pick up my daughter from preschool. I shudder, thinking of how much time I've wasted daydreaming about someone else's life. Don't most people daydream about themselves? What's wrong with me?

But I know the answer. When I daydream about my life, about my career, only good things happen. I book that series-regular gig or lead in a great film. My book sells a million copies. My screenplay wins an Academy Award. And when all of this success is showered upon my head I have all the world's wisdom and levelheadedness to handle it. I take it in stride. I save my pennies. I never sell my soul. We people folk aren't that different from one another, but my imagi-bation never ends with me in rehab, divorced, broke, or as a D-lister on a reality show. It's easy to be self-congratulatory of a fantasy future self. It's easy to say "that will never be me" when it's not.

why do you ask?

THE ONLY CULTURE SHOCK my husband and I felt when we traveled to Ethiopia was when we found ourselves sitting at a dinner table with a group of American Evangelical Christians. They were all from the central and mountain time zones, what New Yorkers and Los Angelenos obnoxiously call "flyover country" (presumably because back when we lived there they didn't pick us for teams, invite us to parties, or ask us to prom, and we're still a bit sour grapes). These were nice people we would never encounter back home. It was good to be reminded that even big cities can be insular; even we cosmopolitan urbanites can be myopic.

After introductions but early in the conversation,

one woman asked, "So, how old are all of you?" After choking on my *doro wat*, I looked up to realize I was the only one surprised. She was not being rude but rather making polite conversation in accordance with the norms and mores of her region.

I smiled. "Sorry if I seemed taken aback. Age is sort of a taboo topic in New York. I have friends I have known for over ten years and I still have no idea how old they are."

"You're kidding!"

"No. But bizarrely, it would not be considered impolite to ask a new acquaintance how much they pay in rent." She laughed, certain I was joking, but it's truer than a blue sky.

However, the top two questions New Yorkers ask upon meeting someone new are not quite as forward: "Where do you live?" (meaning the borough and neighborhood) and "What do you do?" I am fiercely proud of the former, but the latter is a landmine—not so much the initial "So, what do you do?" but the follow-up questions in response to learning I'm an Actor, Writer, Whatever.

I am not a socially inept misanthrope (most days). I can do small talk. Certainly not *all* follow-ups are horrible. The intent matters. Are they just curious? Do they not understand? Or are they assholes?

Luckily, most questions do fall into the just-curious-making-conversation category, such as "Have you been in anything I might have seen?" to which I reply, "Maybe. Did you see the employee training video for the Peninsula Hotel?" Strangely, no one to date has answered, "Wow! That was you!" Instead they pretend they hear someone calling from the other room and politely excuse themselves.

When you happen upon another Actor, Writer, Whatever, the "just curious" follow-ups make for pleasant chitchat, swapping tales from the front, the discovery of common colleagues and the accompanying "What a small world!" But sadly, sometimes that Actor, Writer, Whatever is also an Actor, Whatever, Asshole. They ask the "just curious" sorts of questions to suss out which of you is higher in the pecking order. If it's them they'll weave their résumé into any conversation ("Yes, it has been a warm winter. Reminds me of the time I was on set with Woody—I learned so much about acting just watching him."). If it's you, sit back and watch their head wheels spinning only one thought: *Can this person boost my career?*

Then there are the follow-up questions people ask because they don't understand an aspect of Acting, Writing, Whatever-ing. Which is usually fine, but once

at a New Year's Eve party a guy asked, "I hear you act.
Do you do nudity?"

This was creepy on many levels. First, these were
his very first words to me. Second, this was not a red
plastic cup frat-house kegger but an intimate eight-
guest dinner party. Third, he was there with his wife
and small child.

I was younger and easily thrown off guard then. I
mumbled the standard "If it's not gratuitous and appropriate for the role" answer and then pretended someone was calling me from the other room. The truth is
that the subject has never come up. Ever. No one wants
to see me naked, and frankly I can't blame 'em. Even
my husband prefers the lights off (I'm not buying his
"it screws with my circadian rhythms" bullshit explanation). Not that I'm a grotesque with six nipples on
my ass or anything, but if you're paying premium cable
prices you want to see something spectacular to the
point of inhuman (implants). We all can get "so-so" or
"not bad" in the mirror for free.

Still, the most shudder-inducing follow-up questions fall into the third column: the "question-that-
really-isn't-a-question-but-a-passive-aggressive-put-
down-disguised-as-a-question" question. I met the
champion of this at a friend's engagement party on the

Upper East Side. The fewer people I know at these events, the higher the likelihood of my being seated next to a jackass. This time the jackass was a woman who was an investment banker at Lazard Frères. I know this because she mentioned it nine times before the appetizers.

When she had that properly drilled into us, she began chanting the name of her alma mater as a mantra, including a tale of how earlier that day, while she was sporting a sweatshirt emblazoned with her beloved college crest, a waitress at a coffee shop pointed and said, "Hey, I went there too!" The Lazard Frères investment banker was not at all ashamed to share her first thought: "And you're [just] a waitress?"

"Funny, I thought that was a safety school," I replied. "I mean, it's not like MIT or an Ivy or any-thing . . . but I went to state college, so what-the-philis-tine do I know. Please pass the salt."

I didn't say that. I only thought it really, really hard. Which is regretful because if I had offended her maybe she would have stopped talking. Alas, she didn't tire of herself until mid-dessert. At that point she turned to me and asked, "So what do you do?"

"I'm an actor and a writer."

"So what do you *really* do?"

She thought she was being funny. She knew she

was putting me down. She thought putting me down was funny and assumed I was too much of a moron to realize it. This was a snob of the worst sort and yet the "question" stung me. I hated the truth of it. I wasn't able to earn a living solely through Acting, Writing, Whatever-ing. And I couldn't bear the thought of this woman getting off on putting me down, so I cock-blocked with a lie of omission: "I have a very small role on a soap." I feigned feigning modesty, my tone suggesting the role was big and I was being humble.

Her demeanor completely changed. "Which one?"

I told her. She'd been a fan since junior high. This brought me out of the realm of dim-witted dilettante. Suddenly I was her equal. She eagerly asked if I'd met a certain actor. I had. She squealed like a stuck pig in heat (not that I actually know what that sounds like). I told her I barely knew the guy. The only unscripted contact we'd ever had was a handshake and a "Hi, my name is . . ." but it didn't sink in. She was a million questions at a thousand miles an hour.

"Does he look the same in person? Does he have a girlfriend? Where does he live? Does he live on the Upper East Side? I heard he did. Does he have a girl-friend? Do you ever hang out with him? Do you know where he hangs out? Does he have a girlfriend?"

"I don't know. I just worked with him a few times

and—hear that? Someone is calling you from the other room . . . No really, you better go check."

When she got up I ate the rest of her dessert.

Some people are provocative to the point of trucu-lence with their "question-that-really-isn't-a-question-but-a-passive-aggressive-put-down-disguised-as-a-question" follow-up question, in an attempt to supple-ment their own lack of charisma and confidence. Driven by an assholier-than-thou attitude, they demean others to feel superior by comparison. They are profoundly annoying, but I don't take it personally because it's not personal. These types are equal-opportunity awful. Haters gonna hate.

I do take the "question-that-really-isn't-a-question-but-a-passive-aggressive-put-down-disguised-as-a-question" question personally when it is asked by some-one who is cordial to doctors and ditch-diggers alike but aims their laser beam of bile at me *because* I'm an Actor, Writer, Whatever.

Years ago, I ran into a guy from high school at a bar near my hometown. He was nice enough while we were talking about whom we had kept in touch with, where we had gone to college, and the like. But when the con-versation turned to careers (he was now an engineer) and I told him that I was in town visiting from New

York, and was an Actor, Writer, Whatever, he sneered, "I think you're mistaking your hobby for your vocation."

Yes. I realize that technically that was a statement and not a question . . . and it wasn't passive-aggressive. It was aggressive-aggressive. But he's not alone in his thinking. He was just dickish enough to say out loud what others think or say behind my back—Acting, Writing, Whatever-ing is a hobby, like bird watching or pinochle, and I am both feckless and delusional to thus define myself. High School Guy didn't see that hobbies are fun and work is . . . well, work, even if that work is fun at times. It's the difference between playing baseball in an after-work league and in the minor leagues. The minor-league player may get paid a pittance and never make it to the majors, but he's still a professional ball player. Money, fame, or success isn't what makes the difference between the hobbyist and the professional. It's commitment.

A mindset exists that unless what you do makes money, there's no value in it. Nuns and priests get religious exemptions. But artists, community organizers, and stay-at-home parents are not respected for pursuing their calling instead of pursuing the dollar.

Or perhaps High School Guy believed the stereo-type of the Slacker, Actor, Writer, Whatever: too lazy, irresponsible, and immature to get a real job and grow up. It is true, some people do just that. Some people never put shoulder to wheel, and use the label of "artist" to legitimize partying and prolonging their adolescence. But most Actor, Writer, Whatevers work harder than anyone I know. Hell, I worked at investment banks, and we work a million and a half times harder than those guys—at work that is all encompassing: physical, mental, emotional. Work that is all the time. We are always scanning, always observing, always filing things away, all with our emotions just beneath the surface so they're accessible when we need them. It can be intense. I suspect it's the reason some fall to abusing drugs and alcohol . . . in search of respite from the restlessness.

Or maybe High School Guy (and this may be both convenient and cliché) was jealous . . . harboring some secret dream and envious of me actually pursuing mine. This possibility irritates me the most, because we all have fantasy jobs that tickle our imaginations. I'd be an FBI agent in the vein of Scully on *The X-Files*, but I did not ask the "question-that-really-isn't-a-question-but-a-passive-aggressive-put-down-disguised-as-a-question" question when I met an actual FBI agent, because that would make me petty and malicious (though I was disappointed to hear she had never chased someone down a narrow alley and pointed her gun, commanding, "Stop right there! FBI!"). Even if I were an emotional Neanderthal, there is no need to be nasty because I'm not serious about crime fighting. It's just fun to daydream. The itch is easily sated by a good novel or a noir film.

Some never find a fun outlet for their itches but are too scared to "go pro" lest reality disappoint. They stay safe in a bitter semisweet dreamland where they are brilliant without toil. And at a small-town dive bar, perhaps they'll ask the "question-that-really-isn't-a-question-but-a-passive-aggressive-put-down-disguised-as-a-question" question of someone who actually had the *cojones* to try—only to discover that she *was*, in fact, bad at it. Then made sacrifices, practiced, repeatedly fell on her face—often publicly—and then worked some more, only to be able to stand back and say, "Not brilliant. Just better," before heading back to the batting cages to do it all over again—all the while knowing nothing she does will ever really be done. Nothing will ever be complete. Nothing will ever be perfect.

I should stop whining. As far as problems go, this doesn't even rate. At most it's an occasional annoyance. I've grown more skillful in steering conversations as well: When someone at a dinner party or one of the mommies at the playground asks, "So what do you do?" I simply say, "Oh, I have my finger in a number of pies." If they press further I say, "I'm home with the little one part-time and I'm a philosopher . . . and sometimes I strip . . . on a pole. Not furniture." There is no follow-up.

| the memoir rules!

I AM IMMATURE. At least in regard to my Actor, Writer, Whatever-ing, I am comparable to a two-year-old. Typical two-year-olds don't separate their aims from their means. They'll throw a ball to no one in particular simply because they like throwing the ball. They'll run for the sake of running with no particular destination in mind. It's just what two-year-olds do.

In the film *New York Stories*, the fledgling artist ingénue pleads with her much older lover and mentor, a renowned painter, to tell her whether she has any talent or should pack it in. She is desperate for affirmation, validation, a shred of encouragement. He doesn't give it to her. Instead he tells her what I know to be the truth: it doesn't matter what he or anyone else thinks, "It's yours. You make art because you have to—'cause you got no choice. It's not about talent. It's about no choice but to do it." Artists make art because they are compelled to. They can't stop. At least I can't stop. It is just what I do. Just what I am. Like my being short, there is nothing I can do about it. It doesn't matter if I am good or bad at it, successful or unsuccessful, rich, poor, or destined to die facedown in a gutter. No matter how miserable the circumstance, *it's just what I do.*

Wait a second. Does that sound familiar? Ah yes, I have said that before. In the introduction.

This is what must be so disappointing for you. I didn't follow the rules. In a memoir, even in this memoir-*ish* form, the "journey" should change me. But I didn't change. I didn't grow. I am not better for the experience. Ride the introduction to the conclusion and yep—I'm pretty much the same. No forward movement. No transformation. No redemption.

Take a memoirist who was abused as a child (yes, yes, I know child abuse isn't funny, but there is a slew of I-had-shit-for-parents memoirs). She'll start with said wounding childhood, then tell of her downward spiral into addiction and homelessness; then she'll hit rock bottom, get clean, and by the end find peace and happiness counseling troubled youths. Other memoirs narrate the overcoming of seemingly insurmountable obstacles. Perhaps a poor farm boy couldn't afford a real baseball so he practices by pitching gourds at the heads of scarecrows in the hopes that he will one day become a pro baseball player. He jumps various high hurdles to eventually become the major-league pitcher who throws the final strike that wins his team (underdogs, of course) the World Series—nanoseconds before his mother, who always believed in and encouraged him, passes from her deathbed to the next world, at peace in the knowledge that her boy has "made it." Now those are memoirs. Those are "journeys." Starting and ending in the same place is just plain lame.

Celebrity memoirs also fabulously capture "the journey." They can even make it work brilliantly in its abbreviated form: the celebrity interview. Once in a while I'll happen upon an interview whose narrative begins with the parents who didn't support the celebrity's endeavors. The celebrity gets a little choked up. I holler at the television, *Of course they didn't. They didn't because they are your parents and they love you and being an Actor, Writer, Whatever is a stupid stupid stupid idea!* My preschool daughter is already showing signs of a creative mind and a flair for the dramatic. I put the kibosh on that right quick by sending her to one of those neighborhood learning centers that employ math drills and Maoist brainwashing techniques to squelch every last drop of creativity out of her. Then I switched out her bedtime books from the whimsical favorites *The Cat in the Hat* and *Where the Wild Things Are* to *Allie the Amazing Actuary* and *1-2-3 to M.I.T.*

No parent wants her kid to be eating ramen noodles and living with seven roommates in an East New York tenement when they're thirty-three years old. At the other end of the spectrum, nobody wants her kid to be hounded by photographers, encumbered with the albatross of a public persona, and checking into some fancy shmancy rehab center because of the prescription drugs they've been downing to deal with the mental and emotional pressure. With either outcome they're going to be spending a great deal of time looking for their next job, their next publisher, the next investor for their film.

Good parents want their children to become architects, translators for the U.N., college professors. Stable jobs that are engaging and interesting but allow for time to enjoy family, friends, and hobbies. We want our kids to have easy lives. Sometimes the celebrity interviewee tells the opposite tale, equally teary-eyed: "My parents always encouraged me to follow my dreams. I wouldn't be here on this stage without them." If the celebrity is the seemingly sane sort I think, *I bet you didn't have a bedtime and ate all the candy you wanted too.*

If they're the off-the-deep-end-big-hot-mess-in-a-dress sort I think, *No wonder you're fucked up. What kind of parent wants this for their child? Seriously.*

And still, we're shocked when someone quits.

The other day I was meeting an actor friend for lunch when we bumped into someone we hadn't seen in a while. She had gotten out of The Business. I forgot what she said she was now doing . . . massage therapy? Nutrition? Family counseling? (Many entertainment industry expats leave for the healing arts. This can be a very toxic business.) Whatever it was it became her. She looked good. Serene. After she left I commented to my friend, "Wow, she looks great."

He replied, "Yeah . . . but do you think she's happy?" He wasn't being catty. He really wondered. He was genuinely concerned for her.

I hate to admit it, but I too had a bit of that feeling, though it makes no logical sense. It's not as if she dropped out at the twenty-fifth mile of a marathon we are all destined to win. But for those of us afflicted, who, like the seasoned artist in *New York Stories*, feel we don't have a choice, it's hard not to feel that people like her have been defeated. Have sold out. Have traded dreams for creature comforts. Have lost their balls, and we're the badasses, we Actor, Writer, Whatevers WHO HAVE NOT GIVEN UP.

186 | mellini kantayya

They must be so envious. They must miss this every day. They must be so, so sad to not be sweating their next audition, worried about where their next job is coming from. They must miss terribly getting rejected several times a week, not having the phone ring, not getting the part they really wanted, or having the part they did get—the one they thought would be their big break—cut out of the film. They must pine for the days they wrote screenplay after good screenplay that didn't get optioned, or optioned but not made, or worse—had their story with the tenor of *Sophie's Choice* get milled into a teen vampire flick.

It never occurs to we Actor, Writer, Whatevers WHO HAVE NOT GIVEN UP that those who can quit and do might actually be fine. This business will break your heart. Break. Your. Heart. Yet it never occurs to us that we are the crazy ones. We are the ones who fit the definition of insanity: doing the same thing over and over again, expecting a different result. What we Actor, Writer, Whatevers WHO HAVE NOT GIVEN UP have is dependency—The Business treats us badly, but we get just enough reward to stay hooked and keep chasing the dragon. Many Actor, Writer, Whatevers began pursuing a career in the arts due to some lack in their lives; sure, sometimes the lack was love and attention, but sometimes the deficiency is just a creative thirst. Bully for those people who have the revelation that they can quench it with something healthier than show business. I respect that. I'm jealous they found an easier way to live a gratified life.

Because the truth is, I tried. After one exceptionally trying week, I decided I'd had it. I couldn't take it anymore. I was going to brainstorm alternatives to this botched experiment and come up with a plan. I took out a pen and a fresh piece of paper and tried to think of something—anything—else I could do. After an hour the only thing on the paper was doodles of stick figures in various pornographic poses. I could not think of one single thing. So I crumpled up the paper, had a cookie with a pint of mocha fudge for a chaser, and sat down at my computer and wrote a teleplay. It wasn't a very good teleplay, but writing it made me feel better.

So I don't arc. I don't do exposition-to-rising-action-climaxing-into-denouement. I am a flat line. But maybe, since I'm trudging through a wild and bizarre landscape, that flat line is the right path. Exposition-to-rising-action-climaxing-into-denouement describes the elements of drama. Maybe that flat line keeps the drama on the page and on the stage—in my work and out of my life—leaving me to just keep doing what I do.

about the author

At the end of a book there's often a little author bio. It is usually short—maybe a simple line like, "John Smith lives in Brooklyn, New York." I like those the best, but I've been known to enjoy a slightly expanded bio: "So Andso was born in Korea and immigrated to the United States in 1990. She is the 2010 winner of the Ascot Award for Historical Fiction. She resides in Berkeley, California." Short and sweet. Honest and impressive. We easily follow the unadorned narrative of So Andso's career—she came to the U.S., won a literary award, lives in California. No ambiguity. No affect. No embellishment.

When Actor, Writer, Whatevers are asked for a bio, perhaps for a program or a press release, we're usually told to keep it under a hundred words. That doesn't seem like a lot (the above paragraph is 105 words), but it's too many. I dug up a bio from an old grant application:

> Mellini Kantayya is a writer, actor, and director. She wrote, directed, and starred in the Way-Off-Broadway play, *Intimacy Issues*, which enjoyed a sold-out run. Her screenplay *The Prince of Law and War* was a quarterfinalist for the Creative World Awards. Her screenplay *Enlightened New Jersey* finished in the top 15% of the Academy of Motion Picture Arts and Sciences' Nicholl Fellowship competition. She developed a children's television series, which was the IAMAA's finalist for the ABC/Disney Talent Development Grant. Her independent film credits include *Keane*, *Children of Invention*, and a starring role in *Colin Hearts Kay*.

Not so succinct. I crammed as many minor credits as possible into exactly a hundred words to compensate for the one substantial credit I don't have. And although the bio is 100 percent true and not the slightest bit padded, I sniff for a phantom trace of bullshit. Surely my lack of achievement is transparent. I want to add a disclaimer to each line:

Mellini Kantayya is a writer, actor, and director. *Though she has only gotten paid for one of these things.*

She wrote, directed, and starred in the Way-Off-Broadway play *Intimacy Issues*, which enjoyed a sold-out run. *In a twelve-seat theater.*

Her screenplay *The Prince of Law and War* was a quarter finalist for the Creative World Awards. *And that's as far as it got.*

Her screenplay *Enlightened New Jersey* finished in the top 15% of the Academy of Motion Picture Arts and Sciences' Nicholl Fellowship competition. *And that's as far as it got.*

She developed a children's television series, which was the IAMAA's finalist for the ABC/ Disney Talent Development Grant. *Are you really going to make me go through the humiliation of repeating myself?*

Her independent film credits include *Keane, Children of Invention*, and a starring role in *Colin Hearts Kay. The last being a lovely little film that never got the distribution deal it deserved,*

partly because they cast me instead of a bankable
star to play the best friend.

I eliminated many credits of equal weight in order
to make the hundred word maximum, yet I cannot wax
poetic about how these are all hard-won credits to be
proud of. I cannot depreciate them either. And there's
the rub that keeps on rubbin': I am not a success. I am
not a failure. My career is going well. My career is in the
crapper. I feel authentic. I feel like a fraud. I am proud
of my accomplishments. I am ashamed I haven't done
more. (*She's my daughter!* Slap! *She's my sister!* Slap!
She's my daughter and my sister!)*

But I can deal with the dichotomies inherent in the
Actor, Writer, Whatever life. Actually, it's not a matter
of "dealing" with the life. It just is. Like day is the opposite of night. That's the way my world works. Which is
why I'm perplexed when people ask me what this book
is about. My answer, "It's about not making it in the
entertainment industry," is met with—

Silence.

Then a look. A very-hard-to-describe look. Surprise? Pity? Perhaps the look one adopts while bolster-
ing an uncomely child: *Oh, sweetheart, you'll grow into*

---

* Faye Dunaway in *Chinatown*, biatches. Put down book and rent immediately.

your looks eventually. Really you will. Really . . . would you like a cookie, honey? Or perhaps it's the wiggling discomfort of being cornered by an over-sharer at a work function: *I'm so glad they opened the gym downstairs. After my hysterectomy I stopped working out and my therapist says exercise will ease my depression so I can wean off my meds. Let me tell you, between the depression, meds, and vaginal dryness my sex life is nonexistent and the hubby is non-happy!*

They look at me as a downer. A negative person. I am not a negative person. I am not a positive person either. The glass is neither half full nor half empty, just filled to the midline—about four ounces (if I stumble upon it after noon I may add an additional ounce of vodka and a twist and be on my way). Some do not realize I require no cheering, and accompany the look with a pep talk: *Oh, come on, I'm sure you're very talented. You were on that show, right? See, your big break is probably just around the corner!* These folks won't take "statistically unlikely" for an answer. It's too jarring to their worldview: human beings, at least American human beings, are supposed to have an eternal well of self-confidence and optimism. A positivity so powerful it can override the empirical. We *have* to believe our big break will come one day. Being at ease with any other possible outcome is blasphemous . . . even if it makes us unhappy.

I'm not saying I'm resigned to never having that one stunning bio credit in a miserable-defeated-depressed-person kind of way. I'm actually very ambitious, and though I have never taken one of those happiness quotient psychological quizzes, I suspect I would rate rather high. It's just that *calling* myself "happy" feels . . . garish. I prefer the label "contented." Cool like that. Chill. Ah'ite.

I'd use the word "acceptance" if it didn't trigger my gag reflex, but here I am—equal parts satisfied and dissatisfied with my bio. Sometimes I'll read a line and smile. Like when my daughter beams at her creative insight to adorn her finger painting with purple glitter, or when she bows after an impromptu performance in our living room; I like the joy of the spark and the applause the credit represents. But I am also querulous because of what's not there: projects I'm dying to work on, screenplays I want produced, roles I haven't landed. After all, Actor, Writer, Whatever-ing requires an audience. And nothing gnaws at me more than that script lying dormant in a desk drawer or that perfect-for-me part I didn't even get to read for. Oddly, I am satisfied in my dissatisfaction. Curiosity, restlessness, wanting, and irritation all motivate me. I kvetch but I kinda like the

---

* Ah'ite *adverb* \'ô-īt\ A super-duper hip way to say "alright".

hustle. This is where the clichés work. Pearls are the result of irritated oysters. It takes a lot of shit to grow an orchid.

And it's just as well. If it weren't for the slings and arrows, I'd be left with an overabundance of self-confidence, and rendered the world's most annoying person (I don't even make the top forty now).

But this stuff crosses my mind only during the off hours. When I'm actually working—writing, rehearsing, or performing—I feel nothing. Thoughts of myself disappear. Worries disappear. Delights disappear. Time doesn't exist. Nothing exists but the energizing calm of full absorption and engagement in what I'm doing. Nothing in the world but Actor, Writer, Whatever-ing. Not a *high*, but an invigorating, intoxicating, addictive . . . *middle*. And, really, that's the only About the Author I need to be about. As long as I don't forget that, I'll continue to be a very lucky girl.

acknowledgments

I would like express my thanks to: Devin Keyes, Amy Lopez-Cepero, Megan Canning, Kristin LaBuz, Katy Riegel, Sarah Schmidt, Gillian Williams, Prudence Peiffer and Rowland Stebbins of the Folding Chair Reading Series, and Natasha Dougherty for saving the day.

Lisa Silverman, copyediting goddess.

Wendi Parson for all her support.

Bob Krakower, someone who most definitely *can* teach, and my colleagues in Bob's master class: I can't express how much your honesty, camaraderie, and support has sustained me.

And to:

Sean, for everything.

And, Teru Lily, the funniest girl I know, who teaches me something new every day.

| about the author

Mellini Kantayya lives.*

---

* For now. (See chapter titled "The Antisocial Network," paragraph one.)